To my parents
D'ete and Bill

W.F.P.

To my wife
Sharon

R.H.C.

Cross-Cultural Perspectives in Introductory Psychology

Second Edition

William F. Price, Ph.D.
North Country Community College

Richley H. Crapo, Ph.D.
Utah State University

West Publishing Company
Minneapolis/St. Paul   New York   Los Angeles   San Francisco

WEST'S COMMITMENT TO THE ENVIRONMENT

In 1906, West Publishing Company began recycling materials left over from the production of books. This began a tradition of efficient and responsible use of resources. Today, up to 95% of our legal books and 70% of our college texts and school texts are printed on recycled, acid-free stock. West also recycles nearly 22 million pounds of scrap paper annually—the equivalent of 181,717 trees. Since the 1960s, West has devised ways to capture and recycle waste inks, solvents, oils, and vapors created in the printing process. We also recycle plastics of all kinds, wood, glass, corrugated cardboard, and batteries, and have eliminated the use of Styrofoam book packaging. We at West are proud of the longevity and the scope of our commitment to the environment.

Production, Prepress, Printing and Binding by West Publishing Company.

 TEXT IS PRINTED ON 10% POST CONSUMER RECYCLED PAPER

 Printed with Printwise
Environmentally Advanced Water Washable Ink

Contents

Acknowledgements

I would like to thank all those who have been involved with this project. Four years ago I was notified by the State University of New York that I had received a Faculty Grant for the Improvement of Undergraduate Instruction. This SUNY grant helped this project get off the ground and on its way to becoming this book. At about the same time I had the good fortune to meet John Dworetzky at the National Institute on the Teaching of Psychology in St. Petersburg Beach, FL who took interest in the idea of adding a cross-cultural component to the introductory psychology course.

Along the way a number of people offered their assistance, comments, and encouragement in the development and production of this book who need to be recognized: Teresa Bordeau, David Campbell, Gail Rogers Rice, and Doug Wilmes. Over the past couple of years, Doug Wilmes and I have spent long hours discussing the components and assessment of General Education at the College. His continued interest in increasing the cultural sensitivity of our student has made completion of this project even more important.

The assistance from everyone at West has been tremendous. I would particularly like to thank Steve Schonebaum for his gentle guidance through the first edition. Denis Ralling and Shannon Buckels have been instrumental in the completion of the second edition of this book. Both Dennis Coon and John Dworetzky have been important in their critical reviews at many different stages in the manuscript development.

I'd also like to thank my co-author Rich Crapo for his contribution to each reading. Rich has given this book a greater anthropological depth which will make the material more interesting and meaningful to students.

W.F.P.

Preface

THIS BOOK is an attempt to expose students to other cultures so as to break down ethnocentric thinking and cultural stereotypes. A major goal of these readings is to increase the student's understanding of similarities and differences among the peoples of the world as they relate to psychological principles, concepts, and issues. We hope to show that many behaviors, although outwardly different or perhaps "strange" by our standards, may serve a very important function to other people. And although outright behavioral expression may vary among different peoples of the world, basic human needs and concerns may not. What we hope to show is how the solutions to problems take on the color and flair of the culture, its people, and specific environments.

The design of the book is very simple. Where appropriate and possible in the standard curriculum of Introductory Psychology, a cross-cultural reading or vignette was developed to go along with the traditional material being presented. This vignette, in the form of a 3-6 page reading, is intended to focus on a cross-cultural aspect of the topic rarely examined by students in the introductory course. Further comparison with traditional material is accomplished through the accompanying discussion questions at the end of each reading.

Twenty-five original articles have been put together in this volume to highlight the cross-cultural perspective of psychology. Cultural groups from around the globe are included and examined. It is our hope that by looking at both traditional and modern cultures we can better understand human universals and differences. Groups within American culture are also studied. The recent interest in multiculturalism in the United States has encouraged us to examine such issues as intelligence, social cooperation, and growing older in our own backyard.

As topics are covered one after another in Introductory Psychology, this material is meant to highlight specific examples/concepts that the student encounters. The difference is that we now change the cultural context in which the issue is found. For example, from an historical point of view, we examine whether hunger can be viewed as the primary motive for Aztec cannibalism. Or, as we try to understand the transition of adolescence to adulthood, we examine how initiation rituals in non-Western societies speak to certain universals with which young people must cope. Does moral reasoning development proceed in the same manner in an African culture as it does in perhaps a rural community in the Midwest? And, does witchcraft serve a positive mental health role in societies where it is found?

In this second edition, new articles focus on psychological theory, states of consciousness, motivation, and abnormal psychology. Two readings have been added to the first section of the book on cross-cultural research and theory. To set the tone for this edition, we have described life among an island group called the Dobuans. We hope this article will help students understand how "human nature" is molded by our socialization processes and life circumstances. Many differences described throughout the book can be accounted for by this explanation.

Other new material includes a discussion of the universality of Freud's Oedipus complex, drinking and drug use as cultural phenomena, depression in non-Western contexts, and the collectivist social orientation found among the Chinese.

By reading about specific behaviors and better understanding their functions in various cultures, we hope that the concept "different doesn't mean worse" will be understood. If we can break away from our ethnocentric tendencies, a new broadmindedness may better help us to appreciate other cultures. Behaviors or practices which seem so atypical to what many of us have experienced may not be so different after all.

Culture, Values, and Social Thought

■ Stimulus Questions

How do the conditions in which we live influence our perceptions of human nature? Is it possible that, under certain conditions, paranoia and mistrust of others might make perfectly good sense as the bases for social customs?

IT is all too easy to talk loosely about "human nature." For most of us, it is tempting to assume that there is just something natural, something basic to human nature, in our own habitual ways of understanding or acting. But the real human world is a lot more complicated. You and I are not born fully "human." We come into the world unequipped to survive without the help of others, most especially our parents. Those others, in turn, have had to learn how to do the helping. They, too, were born helpless infants, without language, without knowledge, and without skills.

The knowledge and habits you have developed have been learned over many years, from the patient teaching of parents, from your interaction with your peers, and even from stories you have heard or read about heroes of far-off times and places. These influences have molded you into what you are now. This is what anthropologists call a way of life, or a culture. It was here before you were born. You came to have your way of life, what is now second nature to you, by being socialized.

You conformed to the ways of acting and thinking embodied by your culture. In short, you did not come into this world with a "human nature." You were taught to have the habits often associated with that phrase.

Each culture is a composite of beliefs and values that have accumulated over many generations. Cultures change, and the histories of the changes differ for each society. Various problems confronted by your ancestors determined the way in which they came to think of the world around them, the skills they needed in order to cope, their customs and their feelings and values. The cultural traits acquired among your ancestors were not the same as those of peoples in other circumstances and in other societies. No two cultures are exactly alike, and what people think of as typical of "human nature" differs in different societies.

This is not an easy idea to grasp. Our experience is so limited that it is hard to imagine how varied cultures can actually be. It is hard to believe that "normal" human beings from different cultures can think and act so differently from ourselves. Nevertheless, some of the ideas you take for granted would seem strange in some parts of the world, and some of your most cherished feelings about what is good or bad would be rejected as bizarre by other peoples of other cultures.

To give you a better idea about how much influence our culture has on our nature, we are going to tell you a story about a people different from your own. They are called the Dobuans. The Dobuans are human, and they still exist today. We are going to tell you about how they lived in the 1920s, when they were studied by Reo Fortune (1932). Their way of life made perfectly good sense in the circumstances under which they lived, and those circumstances were certainly different from yours. We have chosen them to illustrate how very different ways of life can be. It is not because their culture is any less "natural" than any other, but simply because it happens to be different from yours. As you read the following story, try to imagine yourself to have been a part of it. Imagine you had been born among the Dobuans yourself, and reared by Dobuan parents, experiencing the things that any Dobuan child would have experienced. Then ask yourself how your ideas of "human nature" would have differed from your present ideas. If your imagining is successful, you will have a better idea of how adaptive we humans can be. You may start to catch the vision of cultural diversity—of which your own current way of life is but one possibility in the whole human spectrum.

The Dobuans lived on a volcanic island not far from New Guinea. They survived by gardening in the tropical forest of their island. Their

basic crop was yams. Unfortunately, the soils of the island did not guar-
antee them abundant harvests. The Dobuans were often hungry. This
left its mark on them, on how they understood the world, and on their
customs.

Because the Dobuans lacked the power to overcome their problems directly, they turned to religion in response to anxieties about the
marginal food supply. They believed that, by practicing the right ritual,
they could make their crops grow. Preoccupation with the yams they
grew was so great for the Dobuans that these vegetables became
imbued with human qualities. Dobuan children learned, for example,
that yams migrated underground each night to visit other gardens until
the following morning. To prevent this nightly exodus, Dobuan garden-
ers attempted to root their yams to the ground with magic rituals, thus
providing some psychological assurance that the labors of gardening
would not be in vain. But at the same time, the belief that yams could
be fixed to the garden plot by magic had a logical implication: yams
from other gardens could be rooted fast to one's own plot. This appeal-
ing idea, if true, meant that the same magic that preserved one's own
yams could be used to steal wandering yams belonging to a neighbor.
Thus, the very religious ideas which provided relief from worries about
hunger caused mistrust of neighbors who might engage in theft of food
through magic.

Now imagine yourself growing up in Dobu. You soon learn that
under the harsh circumstances of competition for limited resources,
everyone except for your relatives is a rival or a potential enemy.
People who were considered related kept to themselves, and each local
community was composed of related families all of whom considered
themselves to be descended through their mothers from the same
ancient ancestress. Thus, the people of other villages—being nonrelatives—were enemies.

Unfortunately, marriage often had to be worked out between a
man and a woman from enemy groups. At puberty, young Dobuan men
would travel to neighboring villages to visit young women living near
the edge of the forest. Marriages occurred at the decision of the young
women's mothers. Having learned through gossip who was seeing her
daughter, a mother might decide that this candidate would make an
acceptable son-in-law. She would initiate a marriage by getting up early
enough in the morning to trap her daughter's visitor before he could
leave. In the presence of her kinfolk, who would cluster around her
daughter's house, she would thrust a digging stick into the young man's
hands when he emerged and tell him to get to work. He was now her
son-in-law, and as such he was expected to clear a new garden for her.
In addition to this work, a son-in-law's life in this wife's village was

not a pleasant one. As an "enemy" nonrelative, he was a convenient scapegoat whenever anyone was upset. If someone broke a leg, got sick, or suffered any misfortune, he might be accused of having caused the harm through black magic. Every other year, the couple alternated their residence between the village of the wife and the village of the husband. Thus the husband and wife would exchange the scapegoat role.

The belief in magic permeated Dobuan life. Not only did the Dobuans believe that magic was necessary for the growth of crops, but also they generally regarded magic as the underlying cause of all important events: illnesses, crop failures, the coming of rains. Even sexual desire and death were thought to be caused by someone's magic. Many peoples throughout the world have believed that black magic can cause death, but the Dobuans went so far as to believe that all deaths were caused by magic. Thus, whenever someone died, his or her relatives regarded the death as a homicide. Naturally, as an outsider, the most likely suspect was the surviving spouse.

Dobuan life was permeated by mistrust. The American concept of "having fun" would have been strange to an average Dobuan. As a matter of fact, Reo Fortune recounted an incident in which he and a Dobuan man visited a coastal fishing village. When the anthropologist joined the villagers around the fire for an evening of song and dance, the Dobuan refused to join in on the grounds that he might be accused of having enjoyed himself when he returned home. Now, all this is likely to be quite different from the customs and lifestyle with which you are   familiar. But we hope you are able to see that the strangeness is due to your having been reared under quite different circumstances. The American style of relaxed friendship and the quest for fun-and-games are compatible with a relatively affluent mainstream economy. They would not, however, have helped you survive in Dobu.

Had you been reared in Dobu during the period described, contemporary American customs and values would seem strange. Indeed they would seem strange to Puritan Americans of three hundred years ago and even to Victorian Americans of the late 1800s if they could have been exposed to contemporary customs. And that is the point of this story. Our ideas about "human nature" are molded by our socialization and our life circumstances. Our common personality characteristics are also molded in this way, as are those of the people of other societies that will be discussed throughout this book.

■ Reference

Fortune, R. (1932). *Sorcerers of Dobu: The social anthropology of the Dobu Islanders of the western Pacific.* New York: Dutton.

■ Discussion Questions

1. Why is the very idea of one "human nature" potentially misleading?

2. In what ways do the Dobuans particularly differ from common North American ideas of what "human nature" should be?

3. What do you think played the greatest role in giving the Dobuans those characteristics? What factors or circumstances most influence a North American's personality?

■ For Additional Reading

Bateson, G. (1936). *Naven: A survey of the problems suggested by a composite picture of the culture of a New Guinea tribe drawn from three points of view.* Stanford, CA: Stanford University Press.

Benedict, R. (1934). *Patterns of culture.* Boston: Houghton Mifflin.

Chagnon, N. (1983). *Yanomamo: The fierce people.* New York: Holt, Rinehart & Winston.

Evans-Pritchard, E.E. (1940). *The Nuer.* Oxford: Oxford University Press.

Fernea, E. (1965). *Guests of the sheik: An ethnography of an Iraqi village.* Garden City, NY: Anchor Doubleday.

Kluckholm, C. (1944). *Navaho witchcraft.* Cambridge, MA: Papers of the Peabody Museum of Archaeology and Ethnology, Vol.22.

Turnbull, C. (1972). *The mountain people.* New York: Simon and Schuster.

The Use of Projective Tests in Non-Western Cultures

■ Stimulus Questions

Are tests such as the Rorschach applicable as measures of personality to non-Western people? If so, how much weight can be placed on test results from people who have no conception of such tests or whose culture's symbolism is radically different from ours?

IT is not unusual to be apprehensive about psychological testing, even if you are an adult student familiar with the concept and perhaps appreciative of its value. Now imagine how members of an isolated or remote group of people who have no written language might react to such tests. Surprise, fear, and suspicion are all likely. The question therefore is raised whether their responses can have any validity.

One instrument that has been used repeatedly in cross-cultural psychological research is the Rorschach (Inkblot) Test, since its proponents claim that it (a) does not require literacy, (b) is not culture-bound (that it is based on assumptions about the world and reality that are part of their Western culture, usually the middle-class versions most typical of professional people), and (c) can be given to people of different age levels (Barnouw, 1985). Nevertheless, some doubt the accuracy of any projective instrument, including the Rorschach, applied to non-Western people.

7

Certainly, establishing rapport with potential subjects and motivating them to participate is one aspect of research that is always more difficult in a non-Western setting. First, there is the problem of *ethnocentrism*, the tendency for any society to look upon outsiders with suspicion. In at least one case this tendency led the locals to suspect the researchers of being employed by the urban-based government to obtain an accurate census of the village so that taxes could be raised. In recent years Third World people have often taken it for granted that American researchers are hirelings of the CIA and have politically nefarious purposes. Such accusations are difficult to disprove when the research itself or its methods make no sense by local cultural standards.

Even if researchers overcome such concerns and establish adequate rapport, explaining the nature of the research may be quite difficult. How, for instance, does one explain the purpose of a Rorschach test in a society where the experience closest to your use of inkblots might be the ritualistic activities of a magico-religious curer? Perceiving your testing in a religious context might bias the responses of your subjects away from personal symbolism toward their knowledge of their culture's mythological symbols. If that happens, you will not be measuring local personality traits the way the Rorschach is intended to. How do you overcome this problem in a society where the professional study of personality is an alien concept? It is doubtful that a perfectly satisfactory solution exists.

If cooperation in the research is obtained in spite of such difficulties, there still remains a more fundamental issue—communication about the task itself. If the psychologist or anthropologist is fluent in the native language of the subjects, then communication difficulties are certainly reduced, although not likely eliminated. But most universities where researchers are trained do not teach many languages such as Swahili, Navajo, or Pidjandjara. It is common, therefore, for an interpreter to be used both to explain the nature of the inquiry being made and to translate the response. The possibility of distortion exists in both directions. Nuances of any language may make accurate translations difficult, and each language is likely to have concepts that have no precise equivalent in the other. This is a central problem in interpreting the Rorschach test, since scores are based on the kind of things people say about the inkblots.

Some psychologists have claimed that the Rorschach is not culture-bound, that it is appropriate for a variety of cultures because the Rorschach inkblots do not create the shapes of objects or symbols that belong to one particular culture but are merely ambiguous shapes. Mere ambiguity, however, may not completely eliminate the problem of culture-boundedness. The interpretation of the Rorschach inkblots was normed with Western subjects. Therefore, responses are deemed normal or abnormal depending on how they match up with the average Western response.

Let's consider an example of the difficulties in interpreting responses in an alien group by standards of interpretation developed in another culture. Among American or British subjects, there are certain responses that are very common for each card. For instance, there is one card that Western subjects often describe as a butterfly or moth and another often described as a bat. Certain cards frequently remind viewers of men or women. These are termed "popular responses." Any normal subject gives a more-or-less average number of such popular responses. Too few might suggest that a subject has failed to learn appropriate and normal ways of thinking about experiences. Too many might indicate less than average intelligence or a lack of creativity. Such interpretations make sense if one knows something about how many popular responses most people tend to give *in the society that the subject comes from.* However, a popular response to a particular card in one society might not be a popular response to the same card in another society.

A simple illustration of cultural problems with the evaluation of popular response is the so-called "Bat Card" in the Rorschach test. It is commonly seen as a bat-like figure by American and British subjects but could not possibly be seen the same way by traditional Eskimos of the northern Thule District of Greenland, an Arctic environment where bats are absent. Similarly, in a hunting and plant-gathering society where all normal members often saw animals killed and butchered as they grew up, it would be normal for them to see dismembered parts of animals in the inkblots much more often than would urban Westerners. For a typical citizen of New York or London, the same number of so-called "mutilation responses" would indicate a morbid preoccupation calling for psychotherapy.

Consider another example of how cultural difference could influence what is a normal or abnormal pattern of Rorschach responses. Reo Fortune (1932) reported a lifestyle among the Dobuan Islanders in which it was considered normal, even desirable, to be suspicious of other people's motives and generally untrusting. The Dobuans who lacked these traits would have been poorly adapted to life among their people, whereas Americans with the same traits might be diagnosable as paranoid.

In fact, researchers have discovered a variety of cultural differences in people's responses to the Rorschach. For instance, the Pilaga

Indians give neither color nor movement responses. Chippewas do make reference to movement but not to color. The Zuñi tend to emphasize small details rather than the wholeness of the picture, as do the Samoans and Algerians. Several reports indicate that typically the total number of responses is lower in non-Western societies than in Western ones. There also tend to be fewer indications of color, movement, and textures in non-Western Rorschach results. Should these differences, all of which have important implications when Rorschach test results are evaluated, be interpreted by standards established in Western countries?

Let us consider some more specific examples from a classic study of Samoan boys by Cook (1942), in which fifty boys between the ages of 16 to 27 who were in training to become pastors took the Rorschach exam. A high percentage of their responses concerned the white spaces within the inkblots. Clinicians generally interpret so-called "white-space responses" as signs of oppositional tendencies since they are relatively rare for Western subjects. But to three-fifths of these young men, white was an important symbol of purity and their favorite color. Is it appropriate for us to apply the traditional explanation of whitespace to these Samoans?

Few of Cook's Samoan subjects gave responses related to texture, a response that is usually interpreted as indicating sensitivity, sensuality, or a desire for contact. A Western subject might comment on the texture of an animal fur or a rug they'd seen in an inkblot, but Samoan society had few such objects. Does this suggest that these young pastors-in-training lacked sensitivity or a desire for closeness with others? It is more likely that the interpretation is culture-bound.

Colors also present a problem in the evaluation of this test. Cook's subjects seemed to give many "pure-color responses," meaning responses that refer only to a color without indicating what the shape looks like. The traditional interpretation of pure-color responses is that they indicate emotional impulsiveness. Should we view the Samoan responses as evidence that Cook's subjects lacked control over their emotions as would have been the case for Western subjects? Cook pointed out, however, that the color vocabulary in the Samoan language was limited. Most Samoan color terms were names of objects whose color was a prominent attribute, in Samoan, "red" was "fire-like" or "blood-like"; "blue" or "green" was "sky-colored" or "deep-sea-colored." It is true that Cook's Samoan subjects used only an adjective when they described a part of the card as "fire-like." But it is a mistake to call such a response a pure-color response in the same sense as when an English-speaking subject merely says "red."

We need to know much more about which responses to projective tests are cultural universals and which ones are unique to specific cultures before we can use them cross-culturally with confidence. Nevertheless, in spite of the limitations that must exist, there is evidence that projective tests such as the Rorschach can be used in a cross-cultural context. That they have some validity is attested to by the comparable results obtained from different measures: For example, some researchers (Miner & DeVos, 1960; Ritchie, 1956) have compared Rorschach results with other data, such as life histories and children's drawings, collected from the same cultures and found very similar pictures of the common personality characteristics of these societies.

■ References

Barnouw, V. (1985). *Culture and personality* (4th ed.). Homewood, IL: Dorsey.

Cook, P. H. (1942). The application of the Rorschach test to a Samoan group. *Rorschach Research Exchange, 6*, 52-60.

Fortune, R. (1932). *The sorcerers of Dobu*. New York: Dutton.

Miner, H. M., & DeVos, G. (1960). *Oasis and Casbah: Algerian culture and personality in change*. (Anthropological Papers No. 15, Museum of Anthropology). Ann Arbor, MI: University of Michigan.

Ritchie, J. E. (1956). *Basic personality in Rakau*. (Victoria University College Publications in Psychology No. 8, Monographs in Maori Social Life and Personality No. 1). Wellington, New Zealand: Victoria University.

■ Discussion Questions

1.   In what ways might a test such as the Rorschach be "culture-bound"?

2.   How might non-Western people's emotional reactions to being given a psychological test lead to questionable results?

3.   How can one decide if the results of a projective test with non-Western people is a valid measure of their common personality traits?

■ For Further Exploration

1.   Psychologists study people's descriptions of the abstract shapes of inkblots. Anthropologists study their visual arts and songs. Folklorists study the stories they tell to entertain one another. Discuss how these different kinds of data have much in common. In what sense might art, humor, recreation, religious mythology, dreams, and folktales all be called "projective" parts of a culture?

■ For Additional Reading

Lindzey, G. (1961). *Projective techniques and cross-cultural research.* New York: Appleton-Century-Crofts. Discusses the uses of a variety of projective tests in different cultures.

How Universal Are Psychological Theories? Freud and Erikson Examined in Global Perspective

■ Stimulus Questions

Are theories developed by Western psychologists applicable in explaining similar behaviors for people from non-Western societies? Does a developmental theory such as Erikson's apply equally to groups other than the one it was originally intended to describe—white, middle-class Americans?

DURING the last part of the nineteenth century, Freud proposed his idea of the Oedipus complex. Those familiar with his developmental theory remember that it is during early middle childhood that a boy develops troubling feelings about his parent of the opposite sex, and that an antagonism toward the same-sex parent arises due to a sense of rivalry and competition. In the course of "normal" development, these Oedipal wishes are resolved resulting in a stronger identification with the father.

Furthermore, Freud proposed that unfulfilled Oedipal wishes and conflicts might appear through the mechanism of dreams. For instance, a boy's jealousy of his father might be expressed in a dream where something terrible happens to his father—death, dismemberment, or some other sort of tragedy. In Freudian terms such a dream indicates a suppressed hatred for the father based on sexual jealousy.

A cross-cultural psychologist might rightfully wonder whether this dream explanation would be appropriate for other cultures or, conversely, whether it was relevant only to Freud's nineteenth century Viennese society (Segall, Dasen, Berry, & Poortinga, 1990).

What would happen in a society where fathers and sons have a different kind of relationship from the one which Freud knew so well and thought commonplace? Such a situation is presented by the Trobriand Islanders of Papua, New Guinea. Historically, among the Trobrianders' *avuncular* society, boys were disciplined by their uncles (their mothers' brothers) rather than by their own biological fathers. It was the uncles' role to guide their nephews through what needed to be learned and thus to prepare them for adulthood. In the 1920s, famed anthropologist Bronislaw Malinowski observed that an adolescent boy might have a dream similar to the type Freud had encountered, but with one important twist: something terrible happened to the boy's uncle— not his father. But why would a boy have suppressed feelings of hatred and a desire to get rid of his uncle? Surely, sexual jealousy theory seems implausible! Among the Trobrianders, the father is the mother's lover, whereas the uncle is the boy's disciplinarian. So Trobriand dreams involving repressed feelings about uncles are not likely to be due to jealousy, but perhaps to something else, such as a nephew's sense of powerlessness with respect to his uncle.

This example leads not only to a questioning of the universality of Freud's theory of the Oedipus complex, but also to a questioning of its accuracy when applied to Western societies. Might Freud have been wrong even with his own cultural group in regard to the interpretation of this type of dream? Do we really know if Oedipal wishes exist? Clearly, before a theory can be accepted as having global applicability, one must examine the occurrence and meaning of a behavior or, in this case, a dream in more than one culture—something that Freud was not in a position to do a century ago. Malinowski's observations suggest that "Oedipal" dreams among the Trobriand representing repressed hostility toward an adult male were not motivated by sexual jealousy but rather by the power which this person exerted over the adolescent. Perhaps the same reason accounts for the dreams of Viennese adolescents about their authoritarian father-disciplinarians.

Segall et al. (1990) point out that Freud overlooked the two conflicting roles fathers played in Viennese society: they were both their sons' mothers' lovers and their sons' disciplinarians. Because these two roles were played by the same individual, it is not possible to say that the Oedipal-wishes hypothesis of sexual jealousy is a more correct explanation than the disciplinarian hypothesis. With information available from only one culture, how do we know that the correct explanation has been chosen? If Trobriand boys had also had nightmares about their fathers, Freud's sexual interpretation of Oedipal conflicts would stand on firmer ground. But since such dreams were not reported by Trobriand adolescents, the Trobriand data suggests that there is at least one other competing explanation. Segall and his colleagues suggest that, although examining a theory in the context of different cultural traditions may not increase its clarity, the process can at least help us avoid errors and generalizations.

Not everyone agrees that Malinowski's observations have demolished Freud's claims about the sexual basis of the Oedipal conflict. For instance, Spiro (1982) claims that strong Oedipal wishes did indeed exist among the Trobrianders and that father-son relationships there are even more hostile than in Western cultures. What then is the answer to this debate? As Segall et al. (1990) suggest, we must examine an even greater number of societies, including both those which are traditionally Western and those which are avuncular, before a more definitive answer can be reached.

Erik Erikson (1950) created a model of human psychological development that differed from Freud's in its shift of emphasis away from conflicts about sexuality to the various psychosocial skills that one must acquire at different stages of life. According to Erikson, in infancy and childhood, normal development requires the acquisition of the ability to trust others, achieve a degree of autonomy, learn initiative, and acquire a feeling of competence. In adolescence, role confusion must be replaced by a sense of identity. This is followed in adulthood by learning to express intimacy through close relationships and later through generativity, which gives a sense of contributing to the world. Finally, in old age, we must achieve integrity, a satisfaction with the life we have lived.

Several studies have been done both to measure and to validate Erikson's theory of development (McClain, 1975; Ochse & Plug, 1986). Ochse and Plug measured personality components as identified by Erikson in more than 1,800 South African black and white men and women. They found Erikson's concepts (e.g., identity, intimacy, generativity, and ego integrity) difficult to define in ways that are easily measureable. For example, what are the components of identity? And, how do we know if someone has achieved it? Some of Erikson's terms are imprecisely defined, vague, and even overlapping.

As with most stage theorists, Erikson, too, proposed that people progress from stage to stage in an invariant order and at specific times in the life cycle. Successful completion of one crisis sets the stage for confronting the next major task (Erikson, 1950). But do all people go through this series of stages in the exact order described by Erikson, or might variations due to social or historical or cultural conditions be seen in this pattern?

The results of the Ochse and Plug South African study raise questions about both the timing of a particular stage of development and the exact order of these tasks. For instance, certain gender differences were observed. Among whites, women in the age group of 25 to 39 appear to develop a sense of identity before men. This may be, according to Ochse and Plug, because developing a true sense of intimacy must precede a sense of identity, not the other way around as Erikson had asserted. As Ochse and Plug state, "It is quite feasible that by sharing and risking themselves in close relationships, people may learn to know themselves, to reconcile their conception of themselves with the community recognition of them, and to develop a sense of mutuality with their community" (p. 1249). Not until this process is complete can a sense of identity be achieved.

Due to prevailing social conditions in South Africa, including minority status, high poverty rates, and fragmented living conditions, black women had a difficult time achieving a sense of intimacy and thus a sense of identity. The black men in the study also did not exhibit a sense of identity until late in life. In turn, this adversely affected black women who still experienced lack of self-definition, lack of intimacy, and lack of well-being far into middle age. It appears that the experience of the "adult years" was one thing for whites and something quite different for blacks. As social conditions change in South Africa, whole groups of blacks may expect to experience a completely different psychological development than they would have had under apartheid.

In both cases described above, questions need to be asked about how universal and how accurate these theories are. In the first instance, questions have been raised about the interpretation of Freud's Oedipus complex, since Freud's particular explanation did not seem to hold up when examined in at least one non-Western culture which had different family-pattern relationships from those in Europe. As for Erikson's view of the stage at which identity is achieved, some interesting questions regarding the role of intimacy (at least with one different cultural group) surfaced which may cause, once we look beyond our own culture, a reexamination of his overall sequencing of stages. Certainly, the door is also open to rethinking the role of intimacy as a determiner of achieving a sense of identity in America.

■ References

Erikson, E.H. (1950). *Childhood and society.* New York: Norton.

McClain, E.W. (1975). An Eriksonsian cross-cultural study of adolescent development. *Adolescence, 10,* 527-541.

Ochse, R., & Plug, C. (1986). Cross-cultural investigation of the validity of Erikson's theory of personality development. *Journal of Personality and Social Psychology, 50,* 1240-1252.

Segall, M.H., Dasen, P.R., Berry, J.W., & Poortinga, Y.H. (1990). *Human behavior in global perspective.* New York: Pergamon.

Spiro, M.E. (1982). *Oedipus in the Trobriands.* Chicago: University of Chicago Press.

■ Discussion Questions

1. In relation to any psychological theory, what is the value of examining it from the perspective of more than one culture?

2. How might Freud's theory of the Oedipus complex have changed had he had the opportunity of comparing notes with Malinowski?

3. Why does Ochse and Plug's research only confuse the issue of invariant stages rather than disprove Erikson's ideas on the development of identity?

How Much Is
Too Much Kayaking?
A Case of Kayak-Angst

■ Stimulus Question

Most Americans think of kayaking as simply a pastime or athletic activity. Under what conditions could extreme sensory deprivation be encountered during this activity, such that an individual would experience severe psychological distress and perhaps even death?

S ENSORY DEPRIVATION or isolation is "prolonged reduction of external stimulation, in either intensity or variety, that produces boredom or restlessness, but is often experienced as profoundly relaxing. (Dworetzky, 1994, p. G-17) For most people severe sensory deprivation is rare, though mild forms may occur while traveling, at work, or even in therapeutic situations. However, a group of Eskimo from West Greenland practice a lifestyle that subjects their men to repeated and severe episodes of sensory deprivation. As hunters, the Eskimo routinely kayak in the waters off Greenland. Some anthropologists have reported that 10% of the males over the age of 18 suffer from a condition referred to as *kayak-angst*, a psychological disorder caused by a condition of sensory deprivation which shares many symptoms with panic disorders and simple phobias (Simons & Hughes, 1985). Others have described this condition as the "national disease" of these Eskimo (Freuchen, 1935; Honigmann & Honigmann, 1965).

According to case reports published by Gussow (1970), kayak-angst typically occurs while the Eskimo hunter is kayaking in a slightly wavy sea with the sun directly overhead or in his eyes. He experiences a lowering of consciousness due to a lack of external reference points, since he is in a "staring" position demanding minimal or only repetitive movements. Most often kayak-angst attacks take place while the person is hunting alone. If the attack is of milder intensity, a hitting of the water's surface with the paddle may be enough to break the trance-like state. Stronger episodes of kayak-angst may leave the hunter totally immobile and unable to right his own kayak should it happen to capsize. Once an individual has experienced this condition, it frequently recurs.

Gussow (1963) has described kayak-angst as a "perceptual and cognitive distortion leading to an initial sense of confusion and dizziness . . . impaired judgement in estimating distances . . . spots appearing before the eyes . . . feeling the kayak is unbalanced . . . sweating, tickling, trembling, hot and cold sensations . . . the desire to move and squirm but is counterindicated by the hunter's fear of excessive movement . . . cold sensations in the lower regions of the body" (p. 20). A pervasive anxiety causes the hunter to fear for his life. He may have the delusion that his kayak is flooding, that the bow of his kayak is rising out of the water and that he will sink, or that his slightest movement may cause him to capsize. Other thoughts may also occur, including the fear of being attacked by animals moving around and under his kayak. If, after an attack, the kayaker makes it back to shore, often with assistance from other hunters, he frequently has headaches and nausea. Some Eskimo, once stricken with kayak-angst, report it to recur every time they go out to hunt. Others report great anxiety at just setting foot in a kayak. Extreme cases have resulted in men giving up kayaking altogether.

Since sensory deprivation is a commonly occurring situation for these why have they failed to adjust better? Gussow (1963) pointed out aspects of Eskimo culture that may help to perpetuate the problem of kayak-angst. First, there is a tendency among these people to withdraw psychologically and physically from threatening circumstances. This is the customary way of dealing with stressful situations involving interpersonal relationships, as well as other difficulties. Gussow suggested that this "give up" attitude makes it less likely that victims will effectively fight off kayak-angst attacks. He asserted that to survive severe kayak-angst, one must not give in to the initial symptoms when the anxiety begins.

Second, the Greenland Eskimo have a strong belief in self-reliance and are extremely reluctant to express feelings of anxiety, helplessness, or pain. Indeed, they tend to deny them. In addition, they fear what they term "unrelatedness" (being ostracized or rejected by family and community) if they demonstrate some unapproved weakness (such as an inability to kayak). Because of these cultural values, the Eskimo did not discuss their problems of deprivation or kayak-angst and were unable to create the social support that might have helped alleviate the problem.

During the past half-century, as the fishing industry has become increasingly mechanized, work crews on larger, motorized boats have replaced individual fishing from kayaks. Except in the far north, kayaks have essentially died out as important economic tools. The individual isolation that was a hallmark of the working conditions for Eskimo fishers and hunters is no longer as prevalent as it once was. Consequently, kayak-angst among most of the Greenland Eskimo has given way to the problems of drug abuse and alcoholism that are more typical of the dispossessed and socially isolated subpopulations of other industrialized countries.

■ References

Dworetzky, J. (1994). *Psychology* (5th ed.). St. Paul, MN: West.

Freuchen, P. (1935). *Arctic adventure*. New York: Farrar & Rinehart.

Gussow, Z. (1963). A preliminary report of kayak-angst among the Eskimo of West Greenland: A study in sensory deprivation. *International Journal of Social Psychiatry*, *9*, 18-26.

Gussow, Z. (1970). Some responses of West Greenland Eskimo to a naturalistic situation of perceptual deprivation: With an appendix of 60 case histories collected by Alfred Bertelsen in 1902-1903. *Inter-Nord: Revue Internationale d'Études Arctiques et Nordiques*, *11*, 227-262.

Honigmann, J. J., & Honigmann, I. (1965). *Eskimo townsmen*. Ottawa: University of Ottawa.

Simons, R. C., & Hughes, C. C. (1985). *The culture-bound syndromes: Folk illnesses of psychiatric and anthropological interest*. Boston: D. Reidel.

■ Discussion Questions

1. What environmental conditions set the stage for a hunter to experience sensory deprivation? Do any similar situations exist in our culture?

2.   Describe kayak-angst clinically and discuss its implications for the Eskimo for normal day-to-day behaviors and economic success.

3.   What societal or cultural conditions perpetrated the problem of kayak-angst for the Greenland Eskimo?

■ For Further Exploration
1.   Find an example of a sensory-deprivation experiment. How does this example compare with the symptoms reported for kayak-angst?

■ For Additional Reading

Honigmann, J. J., & Honigmann, I. (1965). *Eskimo townsmen*. Ottawa: University of Ottawa. An ethnographic description of traditional Eskimo life, including a discussion of *kayak-angst*.

Simons, R. C., & Hughes, C. C. (1985). *The culture-bound syndromes: Folk illnesses of psychiatric and anthropological interest*. Boston: D. Reidel. An authoritative examination of many of the culture-bound mental disorders.

Depth Perception and Visual Illusions: Why Do Cultural Differences Exist?

■ Stimulus Questions

Are illusions merely an artifact of culture? That is, do different life experiences in different cultures predispose people to being susceptible to different illusions? How could being raised in a particular habitat influence how I see the world?

ANTHROPOLOGISTS have always been interested in how people who have different ways of life interpret the world around them. Some anthropologists have had a particular interest in how people interpret sensory data. They have noticed that there are cultural differences in (a) people's skill at recognizing objects from pictures, and (b) the illusions to which they are susceptible. Explanations of these differences have emphasized the role of culture in guiding our understanding of our sensory experience.

Depth Perception

Think about all the years of practice you have had in interpreting two-dimensional representations of three-dimensional objects. Your training began in childhood as you learned to recognize objects from photographs and drawings and also to render them yourself with crayons on paper. It is to be expected, then, that people who have no experience with photographs or drawings would have difficulties interpreting them.

Today, you may take your skills at interpreting pictures for granted. As adults you might not even remember how much practice it took for you to learn your culture's conventions about how to judge the size and shape of objects drawn on paper and how to interpret various types of photographs. You may recall, however, how strange a false-color satellite image of the earth seemed to you when you first saw one. Yet practice enables a person to recognize the land and water boundaries, the soil and plant types, and even the presence of human artifacts that such images portray.

Hudson (1960) illustrated the role of experience in children's ability to interpret depth in pictures. He showed pictures with various depth cues to school-going children and children who did not attend school. The first group generally interpreted the pictures in terms of the three-dimensional relationships between the individual animals or objects portrayed. The unschooled usually described the individual forms but gave little attention to the depth aspects of the pictures. His conclusion was that the experience with pictures and photographs that comes with schooling was necessary for learning to interpret two-dimensional figures as portraying three-dimensional forms.

Visual Illusions

The well-known Müller-Lyer perceptual illusion (figure 1) consists of two parallel lines of equal length, one ending with outward-pointing arrowheads and the other with inward-pointing arrowheads. Europeans and Americans commonly perceive the former line to be the longer of the two. W. H. R. Rivers discovered that Murray Island Papuans (1901) and the South Indian Todas (1905) were not as likely to be fooled by this figure as were subjects from England. A series of studies in 14 different societies (Segall, Campbell, & Herskovits, 1966) revealed a fascinating fact: The people who misjudged the length of the lines lived in societies that built rectangular houses. People who lived in societies that built round or oval homes correctly evaluated the lines. Those of us who grow up in "carpentered" environments filled with regular rectangular objects and straight lines are set up to be fooled by the Müller-Lyer illusion. We are fooled because when we judge the length of lines, we at the same time make the assumption that, when two objects are of the same size, the more distant object is larger. The arrowheads give us the sense of seeing lines formed by intersecting surfaces—such as the lines formed where a wall meets a floor or where two sides of a roof meet—instead of merely seeing two lines. We experience the line with the inward-pointing arrowheads as longer since it seems to portray a line that is farther away than the other line.

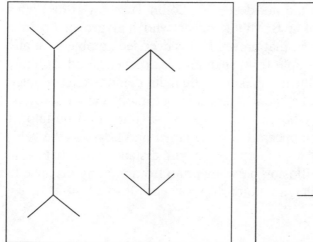

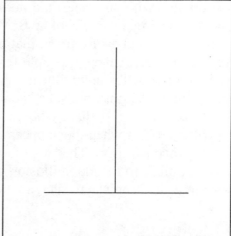

Figure 1   **Figure 2**

Rivers (1901) found a somewhat different result with the horizontal-vertical illusion (figure 2), a figure composed of two lines of equal length arranged to form an inverted capital "T". Both Todas and Murray Islanders had a greater tendency than Euro-Americans to see the vertical line as longer than the horizontal one. Segal, Campbell, and Herskovits (1966) demonstrated that reactions to this illusion could best be predicted by another feature of a people's environment. The most susceptible people were those who occupied territories with broad vistas. They had experienced the visual phenomenon of foreshortening many times in life. They knew, for example, that when a tree or pole falls away from you, it seems to grow shorter, but that when it falls to the left or right across your field of vision its length does not appear to change. So they habitually interpret drawings in the same way. People who have never experienced this phenomenon, particularly those who live in visually restrictive environments such as dense forests, are not likely to be fooled by the horizontal-vertical illusion.

The full-moon illusion also prompts interesting cultural differences in perception. When seen or pictured near the horizon, the full moon seems much larger to many observers than it does when it is viewed overhead in the sky. Segall, Campbell, and Herskovits (1966) found that people who lived in open environments where the horizon was clearly visible were the most likely to experience the illusion of a size difference. Their experience with depth cues associated with the horizon interfered with the accuracy of their judgment. Same-sized objects appear to become smaller as they move away from the viewer and toward the horizon. People who have experienced this phenomenon tend to unconsciously assume that if two objects are of the same apparent size, the one near the horizon must be larger. Those who live in environments such as heavy forests that restricted their experience with such cues are not deceived. Collin Turnbull (1961) cites the interesting example of a BaMbuti archer who had grown up in a densely forested environment that prevented his ever seeing objects at any great distance. Although people from such an environment are less likely to be fooled by the moon illusion, this individual did demonstrate a related perceptual phenomenon. When he was driven on a trip outside the forest he mistook a group of distant buffalo for "insects" or miniature buffalo. It bewildered him when they appeared to grow larger and larger as the vehicle approached them. The lack of experience with distance cues that cause susceptibility to the moon illusion prevented him from relating distance to size in a situation where such a relationship was not illusory!

■ References

Hudson, W. (1960). Pictorial depth perception in sub-cultural groups in Africa. *Journal of Social Psychology, 52*, 183-208.

Rivers, W. H. R. (1901). Introduction and vision. In A. C. Haddon (Ed.), *Reports of the Cambridge anthropological expedition in the Torres Straits*: Vol. II, Pt. I. Cambridge, England: The University Press.

Rivers, W. H. R. (1905). Observations on the senses of the Todas. *British Journal of Psychology, I*, 321-396.

Segall, M.H., Campbell, D.T., & Herskovits, M.J. (1966). *The influence of culture on visual perception*. Indianapolis, IN: Bobbs-Merrill.

Turnbull, C. (1961). *The forest people: A study of the Pygmies of the Congo*. New York: Simon & Schuster.

■ Discussion Questions

1. From the examples of cultural influences on illusion susceptibility, can we conclude that any one culture is superior to another in shielding people from the effects of illusions?

2. The BaMbuti had difficulty in judging size relative to distance but were not fooled by the moon illusion. How does this illustrate that illusions are partially a by-product of some *useful* perceptual skills and not just evidence of a perceptual disability?

■ For Further Exploration

1. Discuss the methodological problems you might expect to encounter in trying to test various explanations for cultural differences in susceptibility to illusions.

■ For Additional Reading

Berry, J. W., & Dasen, P. R. (Eds.). (1971). *Culture and cognition: Readings in cross-cultural psychology*. London: Methuen. A collection of diverse articles that explore relationships between culture, perception, and thought.

Dreams from Culture to Culture

■ Stimulus Questions

How does culture influence what people dream about and how they interpret their dreams? How do the dreams of people in a Nigerian city differ from those of people in a remote U.S. town? Are some dreams and their interpretations universal?

MANY explanations of dreaming have been suggested, from random outbursts of neural cell activity that have no particular meaning, to a process by which the brain cleans out repetitive thoughts to make room for new information, to an expression of repressed desires that surface into awareness during sleep. Whatever the mechanism by which dreams are created, it is safe to say that all people dream, regardless of their culture. However, dreams do differ from culture to culture in two important ways: The content of dreams varies from group to group, and what dreams mean to people is different in different societies.

In its simplest sense, the content of dreams varies culturally because people dream about things they experience in their daily lives. For instance, the Eskimo of two centuries ago had no basis for having dreams that included snowmobiles or jumbo jets. And the dreams of the traditional Zuñi of the American Southwest might have included both desert vegetation and *katchina* rain gods, but not igloos. A contemporary

Canadian's dreams might include religious figures, but probably not the ones that Eskimo or Zuñi would recognize. Whereas Americans and Japanese both experience anxiety-filled dreams about taking tests, the Maasai herders of Kenya and dairy ranchers from Wyoming both have dreams about cattle. In simple terms, people dream about their own realities.

In a more subtle way, there are cultural differences in the content of dreams that reflect not just what is present or not present in a culture but how preoccupied its people are about what they experience. LeVine (1966) studied three Nigerian groups, the Ibo, Yoruba, and Hausa. He found that dreams were most likely to have achievement themes among the Ibo, who were more achievement oriented in daily life, and least likely among the Hausa, whose culture was the least achievement oriented.

Some elements of dreams—those that express basic human needs and dilemmas that are experienced everywhere—seem to be found in all cultures. For instance, sex, aggression, and death are univeral themes. Yet, there are cultural differences about who is most likely to have such dreams, when they are likely to occur, and the specific form they will take. Griffith, Miyagi, and Tago (1958) found that Japanese women were nearly twice as likely as men to dream of killing someone. In the United States it was men who were about three times as likely as women to have such dreams. Schneider and Sharp (1969) reported that dreams of killing among the Yir Yoront, an Australian hunting and gathering group, typically included scenes of dismemberment. Such content is rare in an urban-industrial society such as the United States, where it could suggest psychological disturbance in the dreamer. In a hunting society, it simply reflects common experience.

According to Schneider and Sharp (1969), dreams of death among the Yir Yoront include many cases where dreamers experience their own death, an uncommon dream in American society. Yir Yoront culture includes a preference for marriage between a man and his mother's brother's daughter. It is not surprising, therefore, that Yir Yiront men report recurrent dreams of aggression from their mother's brother, their future father-in-law.

Lee (1958) studied the dream patterns of South African Zulu men and women. The women reported more dreaming than the men, and also more frightening dreams than the men. Men dreamed more often about cattle, particularly about cattle ownership. Women who did have cattle dreams more often had dreams where the cattle pursued and/or gored them. Zulu women also dreamed more frequently of flooding rivers, snakes, and water, symbols that in Freudian analysis are related to pregnancy and childbirth. Those Zulu women who were about to give birth or are having difficulty in bearing children often had such dreams.

Cultural conventions that vary from group to group clearly govern how people interpret dreams. In some societies people regard dreams as real, experiences that they have at night when their spirits leave their bodies. For instance, Biedelman (1963) reports that the Tanzanian Nyakyusa people believed that persons they called *abamanga,* or "defenders," could fight witchcraft-using evildoers in their dreams.

In other societies, people think about dreams as true sources of information though not concrete experiences. Their meanings may not be apparent outside the arbitrary symbolic conventions of the dreamers' cultures. For instance, according to Evans-Pritchard (1956, p. 154), the Nuer, a Sudanese cattle-herding people, believe that dreams may forewarn of death through enactments of death. On the other hand, dreams of death among the Pokomam Mayans imply the likelihood of a long life for the dreamer (Reina, 1966, p. 186). Moreover, for the Nuer, death may be foretold not just by a death scene in a dream but also by the presence of a certain fish, or by the symbol of a walking turtle that the dreamer cannot catch.

D'Andrade (1961) compared societies around the world for their use of dreams as a source of supernatural knowledge and found the phenonemon most prevalent in societies that emphasize self-reliance. Bourguignon (1974) interprets this as evidence that such use of dreams is a response to stresses caused by a lack of human support.

In still other societies, people think of dreams as communications of unconscious wishes of one's spirit to the conscious mind, an idea that was not Freud's alone. The Iroquois of North America are one example of a non-European people who had such a dream theory (Wallace, 1958). For them, hidden wishes of the soul that were revealed in dreams represented deep psychic needs of the dreamer, which could result in psychosomatic illness if not dealt with. Dreamers couldn't always understand the symbols of their own dreams. So they sometimes called upon a religious specialist to help the dreamers interpret the symbols through which their souls' needs were expressed. The specialists entered a trance and used free association or a number of systems of divination to interpret the dreams. Other members of the community tried to help the dreamer fulfill the unconscious need revealed in order to prevent the dire consequences of illness or even death that might otherwise result. Thus, the Iroquois approach to dream interpretation therapy acted as a type of psychological safety valve that allowed unconscious needs to find fulfillment.

In spite of cultural differences in the particular symbols that may be unique to individual societies, there is much unity in the content of dreams across societies. This is perhaps partly because we humans experience similar conflicts, needs, and aspirations, even though they may be expressed differently in each society. Because these similarities exist, there are also amazing parallels in different cultures' ideas about dream symbolism and its role in human psychology.

■ References

Biedelman, T. O. (1963). Witchcraft in Ukaguru. In J. F. Middleton & E. H. Winter (Eds.), *Witchcraft and sorcery in East Africa*. London: Routledge & Paul.

Bourguignon, E. (1974). Culture and varieties of consciousness. *Addison-Wesley Module in Anthropology* (No. 47). Reading, MA: Addison-Wesley.

D'Andrade, R. (1961). The anthropological study of dreams. In F. L. K. Hsu (Ed.), *Psychological anthropology* (pp. 296-332). Homewood, IL: Dorsey.

Evans-Pritchard, E. E. (1956). *Nuer religion*. London: Oxford University Press.

Griffith, R. M., Miyagi, O., & Tago, A. (1958). The universality of typical dreams: Japanese vs. Americans, *American Anthropologist, 60*, 1173-1179.

Lee, S. G. (1958). Social influences in Zulu dreaming. *Journal of Social Psychology, 47*, 165-183.

LeVine, R. A. (1966). *Dreams and deeds: Achievement motivation in Nigeria*. Chicago: University of Chicago Press.

Reina, R. E. (1966). *The law of the saints*. New York: Bobbs-Merrill.

Schneider, D. M., & Sharp, L. (1969). *The dream life of a primitive people: The dreams of the Yir Yoront of Australia*. (Anthropological Studies No. 1, American Anthropological Association). Ann Arbor, MI: University Microfilms.

Wallace, A. F. C. (1958). Dreams and the wishes of the soul: A type of psychoanalytic theory among the seventeenth century Iroquois. *American Anthropologist, 60*, 234-248.

■ Discussion Questions

1. Even though dreaming is universal, why must dreams be understood within the context of the cultures in which they are found?

2.   What evidence is there that the different life stresses experienced
      in different societies may influence the content of dreams and how
      people understand dreams?

■ For Further Exploration

1.   How might cultural differences create problems for the psychol-
      ogist who wishes to use dream contents as a source of insights into
      a patient's psychological functioning?

■ For Additional Reading

Kennedy, J. G., & Langness, L. L. (Eds.). (1981). *Ethos: Journal for the
Society for Psychological Anthropology*, *9*, (4). An entire issue
devoted to articles about the roles of dreams in various cultures.

Alcohol, Drugs, and Religion

■ Stimulus Questions

Is substance abuse purely a matter of individual predisposition toward addiction, or could social conditions increase the likelihood that individuals will engage in problem drinking or drug abuse? How might social customs and institutions make it less likely that individuals will become substance abusers?

SUBSTANCE abuse is a major problem in Western nations today. Differences in rates of abuse suggest that cultural circumstances may play a role in the likelihood that a particular drug will become a social problem. For instance, it has been known for some time that rates of alcoholism differ within different social groups. Snyder (1958) discussed possible reasons for low rates of alcoholism among Jews, and Lin (1953) reported similar low levels of alcohol abuse among the Chinese. The American Psychiatric Association (1994) reports that about 14 percent of people in the United States experienced alcohol dependence at some time in their lives, while 4 percent reported marijuana dependence, and about 1.2 percent have been cocaine-, hallucinogen-, or opioid-dependent.

Horton (1943) examined 56 non-Western cultures in which alcoholism had become a major social problem and found that the higher the level of subsistence insecurity or acculturation was in the societies, the greater was the level of alcoholism among males. This was true, regardless of how much alcohol was present in the drinks were that were available. In other words, in societies in which levels of anxiety were low, drinkers tended to remain sober even when drinking distilled liquor, but where anxiety levels were high, alcoholism was also high, even if the beverages available had only low levels of alcohol.

In 1965, Bacon, Herbert, and Child examined 139 societies and found relationships between anxiety and drinking problems that supported Horton's findings. They also demonstrated that societies with higher levels of conflicts about dependence and independence tended to have higher levels of drinking and alcohol abuse. Societies which pressured children with responsibility and were not indulgent towards children suffered from drinking problems. The same was true in societies which offered little nurturing to adults.

Among the Kpelle of Liberia, "the more rural, economically self-sufficient, and embedded in traditional, older customs was the community, then the lower was the level of what we could call alcoholism" (Erchak, 1992, p. 152). Problem drinkers were most common in the highly urbanized communities and among those most involved in "modern" life. He also noted that "simple small-scale societies, many of whom have used indigenous alcoholic beverages for centuries, only begin to experience significant levels of problem drinking after loss of political sovereignty and economic self-sufficiency. . ." (p. 152).

What are the characteristics of traditional life that might inhibit problem drinking? Field (1962) carried out a cross-cultural study that emphasized the role of those social institutions that he believed helped to control excesses in drinking. He found that alcoholism was less common in societies which continued groups, such as family lineage or clan organizations that owned the means of livelihood and that could punish its members for their heavy drinking.

Similar factors seem to be involved in the role played by drugs in the social life of different peoples. When anthropologists have examined the role of substances which have the potential to be abused in traditional non-Western cultures, they have found patterns of use that contrast with the role of drugs in American society. In many non-Western cultures, hallucinogenic substances have played an accepted role. Instead of simply forbidding their use, societal institutions have seen to it that they were used within acceptable limits.

Grob and Dobkin de Rios (1992) believe that the "cultural contexts of meanings associated with hallucinogenic drugs in traditional societies and with the management of adolescent consciousness states by tribal elders contrast dramatically with American drug use patterns and concepts of the self in western societies" (p. 316). They examined the social controls that inhibit the problem use of drugs in three traditional societies: aboriginal Australians of the central desert region, the Chumash Indians of California, and the Shangana-Tsonga of Mozambique.

In central Australia, traditional aboriginal societies made widespread use of the hallucinogenic plant *Dobosia hopwoodii,* commonly called pituri. This drug contains scopalomine and hyoscyamine alkaloids that induce both hallucinations and illusions. Pituri was widely used to combat hunger and quench thirst. As a hunting aid placed in a water hole, it made animals that drank from the water easier to catch. Pituri played an important social role during a boy's puberty rituals. To achieve social recognition as adults, boys had to pass through a rigorous period of religious training. During a year of isolation from areas visited by women and children, boys underwent religious training and painful ordeals including floggings, scarification, and genital operations. Pituri was used as an anesthetic during circumcision and subincision (surgical slitting of the underside of the penis to the urethra). Pituri was also used during sacred instruction by elders to help boys experience the world. When they returned to ordinary life after this training, the boys had achieved manhood.

The Chumash Indians of California were foragers who survived by acorn gathering, fishing, and hunting. They used the powerful hallucinogenic *Datura meteloides.* Datura was used at puberty as part of the vision quest in which young men sought their personal guardian spirit. In many California tribes, datura was taken in groups, under the direction of elders who instructed the youths in the religious lore, sacred songs, and dances of their society. Among the Chumash, a specialist, assisted by four other elders, gave it to individual men and women at puberty. The datura was treated as sacred and administered during a period of fasting and purification through ascetic practices such as sweat baths and bathing in ice-cold water. The elders lectured the young person about moral obligations while he or she was in a hypersuggestible state due to the influence of the drug.

The Shangana-Tsonga have been described by T.F. Johnson (1972, 1976, 1977). Members of a horticultural society, they number about 1.2 million in Mozambique and about 700,000 in northern Transvaal. Women are the primary food producers, but the land is arid and infertile, so food production is difficult and unreliable. Women have an infertility rate of about 30%, and about 35% of children die before their first birthday. *Datura fatuaosa* is used in conjunction with fertility rituals that are mandatory for adolescent girls. The visions caused by the datura are believed to be manifestations of the fertility deity.

The Shangana-Tsonga fertility rituals are conducted after the harvest in a group setting. While they are under the influence of the drug, the girls are encouraged to experience the voice of the fertility god. By completing the rituals, the girls enter into the status of adult women and are seen as ready to undertake the demands of life.

In the opinion of Grob and Dobkin de Rios, the drugs used in aboriginal Australia and among the Chumash and the Shangana-Tsonga, as well as among many other traditional societies, were not subject to abuse. The supportive institutional environment in which they were used in an acceptable way and the sacred meanings associated with their use prevented abuse. This is in marked contrast with substance abuse by adolescents and young people in the United States. Drug use in this case occurs alone or within peer groups rather than under the guidance of family and respected members of the community. Furthermore, the drug use itself leads to further estrangement from an already impersonal society. According to Shedler and Block (1990), drug education could be effectively carried out through sensitive and empathetic parenting and efforts to promote childhood self-esteem, sound interpersonal relations, and meaningful life goals. These characteristics are found when drugs are used acceptably in traditional societies. They are conspicuously absent in the more impersonal life found in the United States.

■ References

American Psychiatric Association. (1994). *Diagnostic and statistical manual of mental disorders* (4th ed.). Washington, D.C.: Author.

Bacon, M.K., Herbert, B., & Child I.L. (1965). A cross-cultural study of drinking: II. Relations to other features of culture. *Quarterly Journal of Studies on Alcohol*, (Suppl. No. 3).

Erchak, G.M. (1992). *The anthropology of self and behavior.* New Brunswick, NJ: Rutgers University Press.

Field, P.B. (1962). A new cross-cultural study of drunkenness. In D.J. Pittman and C.R. Snyder (Eds.), *Society, culture and drinking patterns.* New York: Wiley.

Furst, P.T. (1972). *Flesh of the gods: The ritual use of hallucinogens.* New York: Praeger.

Grob, C.S., & Dobkin de Rios, M. (1992). Hallucinogens, managed states of consciousness, and adolescents: Cross-cultural perspectives. *Journal of Drug Issues, 22,* 121-138.

Horton, D. (1943). The functions of alcohol in primitive societies: A cross-cultural study. *Quarterly Journal of Studies on Alcohol, 4,* 292-303.

Johnston, T.F. (1972). *Datura Fatuaosa*: Its use in Tsonga girls' initiation. *Economic Botany, 26,* 340-351.

Johnston, T.F. (1976). Power and prestige though music in Tsongaland. *Human Relations, 27,* 235-246.

Johnston, T.F. (1977). Auditory driving, hallucinogens, and music-color synesthesia in Tsonga ritual. In B.M. du Toid (Ed.), *Drugs, rituals, and altered states of consciousness.* Amsterdam: Balkema Press.

Lin, T. (1953). A study of the incidence of mental disorder in Chinese and other cultures. *Psychiatry, 16,* 313.

Shedler, J., & Block, J. (1990). Adolescent drug use and psychological health. *American Psychologist, 45,* 612-630.

Snyder, C. (1958). *Alcohol and the Jews.* Glencoe, IL: Free Press.

■ Discussion Questions

1. What social conditions seem to contribute most often to alcohol and substance abuse? What psychological conflicts and anxieties seem most conducive to substance abuse?

2. What conditions in nonindustrialized societies have been most effective in preventing the abuse of drugs?

■ For Further Reading

Block, P.K. (Ed.). (1994). *Psychological anthropology.* Westport, CT: Praeger.

Myerhoff, B. (1976). *Peyote hunt: The sacred journey of the Huichol Indians.* Ithaca, NY: Cornell University Press.

The Ifaluk Ghosts of Micronesia

■ Stimulus Question

What societal dynamics could account for children and adults alike believing in "ghosts"?

BELIEFS and expectations powerfully affect how one interprets the world. Three types of beliefs that have been categorized are: (a) descriptive and existential, (b) evaluative, and (c) prescriptive or proscriptive (Rokeach, 1973, p. 7). These beliefs may be true or false, good or bad, desirable or undesirable. Everyone holds hundreds of different beliefs. Of course, some are more important than others, and certain beliefs are pervasive throughout a society and apparent in the daily activities and thoughts of both adults and children. How do people acquire such central beliefs? And if they are irrational, such as a fear of ghosts, why do people adopt them generation after generation?

According to Spiro (1967) ghosts are very real to the Ifaluk of the Central Carolines in Micronesia. For about 250 people whose existence depends on fishing and horticulture, the belief in ghosts, both benevolent and malevolent, begins in childhood and continues throughout life. Of greatest importance are the malevolent ghosts that the Ifaluk call *alus*. These ghosts are believed to cause illness indiscriminately throughout the population and are thus feared and hated. Furthermore, they are regarded as responsible for any immoral behavior committed by an Ifaluk. The numerous ceremonies and rituals that focus on the alus is evidence of the Ifaluk's preoccupation with them.

How have the Ifaluk come to believe in the alus and why have they become so preoccupied with these ghosts? According to Spiro, we need better explanations of such beliefs than have been offered by traditional learning theory. Historically, Hullian learning theory suggested that behavioral change occurs due to habitual response to a particular stimulus. But acquiring knowledge about the alus ghosts is not a matter of changing a behavior. The Ifaluk, at a very early age, already accept this belief. They believe they have abundant information to confirm these ghosts' existence.

Another learning-theory approach emphasizes the concepts of drives and rewards. According to Miller and Dollard, a drive is learned through the process of associating a neutral stimulus with an unconditioned stimulus. People learn a secondary drive of fear when a neutral stimulus is associated with a fear-producing unconditioned stimulus. However, Ifaluk children do not learn in any formal way about the alus. The belief is implicit throughout their culture and underlies Ifaluk ideology.

Spiro suggests perception theory as a more useful explanation for the formation of this belief. If people believe that the world is a harsh, threatening place, they will be more likely to develop a belief in threatening objects or forces as the Ifaluk have done. The reverse of this orientation is equally true. Thus, when child-rearing customs create a disposition in most children to perceive the world in the same terms as one another, their similar outlook lends itself to shared beliefs about why life is the way it seems to be. Ifaluk culture standardizes and perpetuates a way of interpreting the world that fits neatly with childhood experiences.

Our beliefs about the world create a frame of reference that then colors our perception of events taking place. To best explain why the Ifaluk would develop a frame of reference wherein they believe in good and bad ghosts, one needs to look at their early childhood experiences. Abundant literature exists on how early life experiences affect later personality development. According to Spiro, Ifaluk children came to develop their world view, which was also that of their parents, from two specific practices affecting their early life.

In Ifaluk culture, parents immediately addressed every need a child had. The mother provided the infant with constant care and attention. People never left very young children alone or allowed them to continue in a state of distress. However, one Ifaluk practice appeared at odds with this infant-centered practice: the daily morning bath. At birth and throughout infancy, parents bathed the child every morning in the very cold water of the lagoon. Adults waited until much later in the day, when the water was warmer, to bathe themselves. The immersion in the cold water was both painful and threatening to the child and was accompanied by constant crying. The experience was in sharp contrast to how the rest of the infant's needs were met. During the bath, parents paid no attention to the infant's cries, and the child, of course, had no control over this unpleasant situation. So, from the first day of life, the Ifaluk child receives two very different messages: first, that the world is a wonderful, comfortable place where one's every need is taken care of, and second, that it is an equally threatening and painful world in which to live. The frame of reference the child acquired suggested that the world could be both satisfying and threatening. The Ifaluk are thus predisposed, at least in part, from infancy to believe in threatening ghosts.

A second event further developed the Ifaluk child's frame of reference in this direction. At the birth of a younger brother or sister, parents rather abruptly shifted their attention away from the older child and directed the bulk of it toward the infant. Previous close attentiveness to their needs gave Ifaluk children very little ability to tolerate frustrations. When their needs stopped being immediately addressed, their frustrations increased, and they perceived the world as threatening. The Ifaluk described children as becoming "ill" at the birth of a sibling because of their intense frustration over the loss of attention. Thus they experienced both security and insecurity, pleasure and pain, and assurance and threat. Children's mixed perception of life made it easy for them to accept the cultural belief in malevolent and benevolent ghosts. The contrasting life experiences of having needs fulfilled and needs ignored predisposed Ifaluk children to develop a dichotomous frame of reference that reflected their inner security and insecurity. Ifaluk ghosts fit very nicely into this conception of the world as both threatening and gratifying.

According to Spiro, the reasons why the adult Ifaluk continued to believe in ghosts could be found in their personality structure. The ethic of nonaggression was supremely important; all overt aggression was forbidden. Even thoughts of hostility toward others were the source of great personal anxiety. To reduce this anxiety, the Ifaluk disowned their own hostilities by projecting them onto the alus. People, by nature, were good. Hostility, therefore, was forced on them by the alus. A belief in the existence of evil ghosts allowed the Ifaluk to maintain their positive beliefs concerning human nature and thus was important to their mental well-being.

■ References

Rokeach, M. (1973). *The nature of values*. New York: The Free Press.

Spiro, M. E. (1967). Ifaluk ghosts: An anthropological inquiry into learning and perception. In R. Hunt (Ed.), *Personalities and cultures: Readings in psychological anthropology* (pp. 238-250). Garden City, NY: Natural History Press.

■ Discussion Questions

1.   Describe the roles assigned to ghosts by Ifaluk people.

2.   How does learning theory attempt to explain a belief in ghosts?

3.   How did the Ifaluk's world view promote belief in the alus? How did children acquire a dichotomous perspective about their environment?

4.   Why did a belief in evil ghosts fit in with the Ifaluk view of human nature?

■ For Further Exploration

1.   Find an article related to a group such as the Amish or the Hutterites. Identify a frame of reference associated with this group and enumerate beliefs that stem from such a point of view.

■ For Additional Reading

Whiting, J. W. M., & Child, I. L. (1953). *Child training and personality: A cross-cultural study*. New Haven, CT: Yale University Press. A classic study of the roles of various cultural institutions in the shaping of personality.

How Children Think: An Issue of Content and Measurement

■ Stimulus Question

How much difference does culture make in how and when a child is able to perform certain mental functions?

CHILDREN are not born with the mental skills of adults; they must develop them. One insight that young children lack is that the number of objects stays the same no matter how they are arranged. Another is that the volume of a liquid remains constant regardless of the shape of the container into which it is poured. The ability to think of number and volume as constants when arrangement or shape is changed was called *conservation* by Piaget (Flavel, 1963), the theorist who first studied the development of this mental skill. Other researchers have undertaken cross-cultural studies to determine whether children acquire an awareness of conservation of number and volume at the same ages in different cultures.

Many such cross-cultural studies have reported that the ability seems to arise somewhat later in non-Western children (Ashton, 1975; Dasen, 1972). Some researchers have tried to discover whether schooling plays a role in how early the conservation skill arises, but the results have been very inconsistent. Some studies (Furby, 1971) have even found that children with less schooling achieved this skill sooner!

One psychologist who has studied the development of conservation in non-European children is Nyiti (1976), who compared Meru tribal children in Tanzania with European children. Nyiti's study has also shed light on important issues about experimental methodology in cross-cultural research. Nyiti noted that the way research is conducted can affect its results. Therefore, poor methodology might be the reason cross-cultural studies have generally reported lags in non-Western children's development of conservation skills. For instance, Kamara (1971) demonstrated in a study of children from Sierra Leone that when the experimenter was a native speaker of the language, no lags were found. The slow development only seemed to be present to researchers who did not speak the children's language.

Nyiti also noted that a recurring problem in doing research on developmental skills in non-Western societies was the difficulty in determining the age of the children. In many non-Western societies it is not customary to keep an exact count of children's ages. Much research about the cognitive development of non-Western children describes their progress based on estimates of age. If the estimates are incorrect, then studies that suggest there are developmental delays in non-Western children's cognitive skills may well be in error. Nyiti attempted to improve the approximation of children's ages by several measurement methods, such as (a) placing children's year of birth in respect to various "Great Events" that people remembered and (b) making "sibling comparisons" to assess more accurately each child's exact age.

Nyiti assessed conservation skills in regard to substance, weight, and volume. To judge substance-conservation skill, he took two equal-sized clay balls and molded one of them into a banana shape while the children watched. The children had to decide if one of the clay shapes was now larger than the other. Weight-conservation experiments required children to judge which was heavier, the round clay ball or the banana-shaped piece of clay that had been molded from a similar round clay ball. To judge volume-conservation skills, Nyiti asked the children whether the water in a glass would rise more, less, or the same amount if the banana-shaped piece of clay were dropped in it instead of the clay ball.

Meru children demonstrated a level of substance-conservation skill similar to that of middle-class European children. Schooling did not appear to speed up the learning of conservation skills. In fact, unschooled Meru children did better on conservation of weight and volume than did their counterparts in school.

Nyiti's research strengthens Piaget's claim that certain mental operations are universal and that they develop in an invariant order at specific ages. Earlier studies that claimed to have found time lags in the development of conservation skills in non-European children were likely flawed with a methodological problem in estimating the ages of non-European children. When Nyiti evaluated the ages of Meru children more carefully, the supposed developmental lag disappeared. His study adds more evidence that children around the world are more similar than different from one another in the development of cognitive skills.

■ References

Ashton, P. T. (1975). Cross-cultural Piagetian research: An experimental perspective. *Harvard Educational Review*, *45*, 475-506.

Dasen, P. R. (1972). Cross-cultural Piagetian research: A summary. *Journal of Cross-Cultural Psychology*, *3*, 23-39.

Flavel, J. H. (1963). *The developmental psychology of Jean Piaget*. Princeton, NJ: Van Nostrand.

Furby, L. (1971). A theoretical analysis of cross-cultural research in cognitive development: Piaget's conservation task. *Journal of Cross-Cultural Psychology*, *2*, 241-255.

Kamara, A. (1971). *Cognitive development among Themne children of Sierra Leone*. Unpublished doctoral dissertation, University of Illinois at Urbana-Champaign.

Nyiti, R. M. (1976). The development of conservation in the Meru children of Tanzania. *Child Development*, *17*, 1122-1129.

■ Discussion Questions

1. How do Meru children differ in conservation abilities from European children?

2. Identify the reasons why the methods used to conduct cross-cultural research are particularly critical if the research is to be valid.

■ For Further Exploration

1. Design a study to determine at what age children acquire the skill of conservation of weight, the principle that the weight of objects remains constant unless something is added or taken away from them.

■ For Additional Reading

Berry, J. W., & Dasen, P. R. (Eds.). (1974). *Culture and cognition: Readings in cross-cultural psychology*. London: Methuen. A classic collection of articles on the cross-cultural study of cognition.

Triandis, H. C., & Heron, A. (Eds.). (1981). *Handbook of cross-cultural psychology: Developmental psychology (Vol. 4)*. Boston: Allyn and Bacon. Summarizes cross-cultural research findings about cognitive development to 1981.

Who's Afraid of a Test? Culture, Gender, and Socioeconomic Status Differences in Test Anxiety

■ Stimulus Questions

Are there racial differences in test anxiety? What effect do gender and socioeconomic status have on the amount of test anxiety shown by U.S. and Chilean students?

TEST ANXIETY, an unpleasant emotional response to being evaluated in a classroom, is a common experience. It is often accompanied by physical manifestations characteristic of fear, such as rapid, shallow breathing. Is it any surprise that severe test anxiety can undermine your performance on a test? A certain amount of anxiety can help performance, but too much usually impairs it.

Recently, Guida and Ludlow (1989) conducted a cross-cultural study of test anxiety in U.S. and Chilean seventh- and eighth-grade students. When they compared test-anxiety scores along culture, gender, and socioeconomic lines, they found significant differences on all three dimensions. U.S. students had lower test anxiety than Chileans; boys lower than girls; and higher-socioeconomic students lower than lower-socioeconomic students.

Guida and Ludlow found Chileans, lower-socioeconomic status students, and women to be more anxious than North Americans, higher-socioeconomic status students, and men. In all but one comparison examined by Guida and Ludlow, males were less test anxious than females. Could certain socialization or acculturation factors explain the lower anxiety in male students? Some research suggests that historical conditions can cause females to experience a "fear of success" (Wade & Tavris, 1990, p. 374). Perhaps test anxiety is simply one manifestation of a more general fear of success.

Guida and Ludlow suggest that cultural differences (U.S. vs. Chilean) in test anxiety may arise because of the different societal significance of tests. When much of your future rides on the outcome of an examination, you are likely to have a lot of anxiety. For example, to gain admission to a university in France, French students must pass the BAC, a national examination given at the end of their secondary education. Japanese high school students also undergo a rigourous national examination that determines where, in the hierarchical university system, they will be placed. A degree from a prestigious university is much more important in Japan than in the U.S. and a better indicator of the student's future socio-economic class. The pressure is intense, therefore, especially from the student's family. Pressure to this extent is generally not part of test-taking in U.S. schools.

When Guida and Ludlow looked at socioeconomic class, they found some interesting cultural and subcultural differences. Middle- and upper-class students from the U.S. had lower test anxiety than did the Chilean students in the same categories. But U.S. students of low socioeconomic class—all of whom in the study were African-American inner-city children—had higher test anxiety than Chilean students of similar class.

Clawson, Firment, and Trower (1981) did an earlier study that helps distinguish the effects of class from race as regards anxiety. They examined differences between *state anxiety*, which is prompted by a particular situation, and *trait anxiety*, which needs no prompting but seems to be a personality trait. Black and white children in Florida (seventh- and ninth-graders) were compared on state and trait anxiety and on their math and language test scores and grade point averages. They differed on all three measures of academic performance and on both types of anxiety. Overall, black children had lower math and language test scores, lower GPAs, and significantly higher levels of trait and state anxiety. But was this really a racial difference? The researchers suspected that the differences were really due to economic class. They noted, for instance, that all students who had high anxiety scored significantly less well on math and language. Those who had high *trait* anxiety were especially low in their GPAs. And these relationships were the same for both races.

When matched for socioeconomic backgrounds, however, the students showed no black-white differences in GPA, trait anxiety, or overall anxiety. But black students were more likely to have high state anxiety than whites (29% vs. 14%). Whites had a much greater problem than blacks with poor performance due to too little anxiety.

From these studies, we can see that upper-socioeconomic-class students tend to have less test anxiety than lower-socioeconomic-class students, giving the former an advantage in test performance (except for those who exhibit too little anxiety). Since whites tend to have a higher socioeconomic background than blacks in the United States, there appears to be a hidden advantage here for white students.

Scarr has shown that when environments are comparable, IQ differences between black and white children all but disappear (see Chapter 19, "Race, Culture, and IQ"). Apparently, the same might be true for differences in test anxiety. Within the United States, therefore, differences are less an issue of race or ethnic background than they are a matter of opportunity and appropriate environment conducive to success and academic attainment.

■ References

Clawson, T. W., Firment, C. K., & Trower, T. L. (1981). Test anxiety: Another origin for racial bias in standardized testing. *Measurement and Evaluation in Guidance, 13*, 210-215.

Guida, F. V., & Ludlow, L. H. (1989). A cross-cultural study of test anxiety. *Journal of Cross-Cultural Psychology, 20*, 178-190.

Wade, C., & Tavris, C. (1990). *Psychology* (2nd ed.). New York: Harper & Row.

■ Discussion Questions

1. What social factors seem to increase children's test anxiety?

2. How do state and trait anxiety affect a person's test-taking performance?

3. What are the pros and cons of using race as a variable in psychological research such as the study of test anxiety?

■ For Further Exploration

1. Imagine that you had grown up in a society that considered you to be a "minority." How might your experiences in life lead you to develop severe anxiety in situations where you know your performance will be evaluated?

■ For Additional Reading

May, R. (1977). *The meaning of anxiety*. New York: Norton. Originally published in 1950, this classic text examines the positive as well as negative aspects of anxiety from the points of view of philosophy, psychology, and psychotherapy.

A World of Colors: Culture Influencing Linguistic Needs

■ Stimulus Questions

How does the semantic richness of a language's vocabulary reflect the relative importance of different parts of a culture? Do different cultural needs shape the languages of different peoples?

PERIWINKLE, burnt umber, lemon yellow, salmon, spring green—these are all colors familiar to any American child who has ever had a box of 64 Crayola crayons. At one time Crayola even marketed a box of 128 colors. You can find examples of the American fascination for colors in many other places. For instance, walk past any cosmetics counter. You'll find more shades of red than you might have thought possible, and probably more than you've ever learned to identify by name. Shocking watermelon, mulberry glow, snowsilver plum, electric red, and raspberry wine don't even scratch the surface of the elaborate list of different colors that lipstick marketers have invented.

In the English language there are over 3,000 words for colors without even counting "shocking watermelon" or its relatives. Our culture appears to have created a very large number of color terms. This is because our technology can manufacture products with very small color differences between similar items. And it is profitable to market products on the basis of these small color differences. Do all cultures cause their languages to become enriched in areas that are important in daily life? It appears so.

In language, a basic category of meaning that becomes elaborated into many words that denote slight differences within the category is called a semantic domain. (Peoples & Bailey, 1991, p. 56). For instance, we English speakers typically use only nine basic color terms. They're the ones that correspond to the nine colors in a small Crayola crayon pack: red, orange, yellow, green, blue, purple (or violet), brown, white, and black. The rest of the 3,000 or more English color terms are merely embellishments on these nine semantic domains of color. The English semantic domain of "blue" for example contains many other terms, such as aqua, sky, royal, teal, cobalt, Prussian, and maybe even a "shocking navy" eyeshadow on some cosmetic counter somewhere.

Of course, elaborate semantic domains don't involve just colors. They develop in any area of life that is culturally important to a society. The Eskimo have many different terms that belong to the semantic domain of "ice," a fairly limited category for most English speakers. For Eskimo, survival has depended on recognizing subtle differences between various kinds of ice. According to Nelson (1969, pp. 398–399) the Ulgunigamiut Eskimo of Wainwright, Alaska, distinguished between *ugurugüzak*, ice in its earliest stage of freezing that causes ripples to disappear; *pogozak,* slush ice formed by the grinding that occurs along places such as ice floes; and *mogozak*, pogozak frozen solid. The Ulgunigamiut also had a name for circular pieces of young ice (*migalik*) and thin, flexible sheets of newly formed ice that seals could still break through to form breathing holes (*salogok*). Believe it or not, the Ulgunigamiut also had more than 160 other names for kinds of ice. Keeping track of that many differences was important to their hunting life in the Arctic. Fine distinctions between kinds of ice were so important to survival in the Arctic that Nelson devoted five chapters—over 130 pages—to the topic in his book about the Wainwright Eskimo.

A similar development of vocabulary richness exists in various other semantic domains. Consider the Dobuan Islanders who lived near New Guinea. Their survival depended on their ability to raise yams in a difficult environment, so they distinguished between yams at various stages of development, size, and ripeness. The Nuer, a pastoral society in the Sudan, had many terms for cattle, the animal on which they depended for their livelihood. In the same vein, cattle ranchers from Wyoming also have many words for the domain of "cattle." They distinguish between "bulls," "steers," "heifers," "calves," and "doggies"—all of which are just "cows" to most U.S. urbanites. Horses may be "foals," "colts," "fillies," "stallions," "studs," "geldings," or "mares."

The work of anthropologist H. C. Conklin (1955), who studied the Hanunóo people of Midori Island in the Philippines, supports the idea that cultural demands are the driving force behind the linguistic richness of certain semantic domains. Their color classification would put Crayola out of business. Their biggest box of crayons would contain only white, black, red and green. So unimportant are color distinctions in the daily life of the Hanunóo that their language even lacks the word "color." To find out a Hanunóo color word for something, you would have to ask it in a roundabout way, such as, "How is it to look at?" Odds are that you would get a description of size or shape well before you were told either *mabiru* (dark, black), *malagti* (light, white), *marara* (red, reddish, dry), or *malatuy* (green, greenish, wet/growing). In Hanunóo, black, violet, indigo, blue, dark green, dark gray, and deep shades of other colors are all *mabiru*. Whites and any light tint of other colors are all *malagti*. *Marara* refers to anything maroon, red, orange or yellow, and most of what we might call earth tones. Finally, *malatuy*, for light greens, or mixtures of green, yellow or brown, designates forest tones, the colors of growing things. The Hanunóo world of colors is really one of day, night, earth, and forest—that is, it describes the world that is important to them.

Some years ago, some anthropologists and psychologists wondered if peoples who had such limited color vocabularies were unable to see color differences. To test this hypothesis, one researcher compared the Dani, a Stone Age gardening people who live in New Guinea, to persons who spoke English (Rosch, 1973). In the Dani language there were only two color words, *mola* for bright warm colors, and *mili* for dark, cold colors. Rosch discovered that the Dani could recognize a variety of colors as well as we can even though they had no words for them in their language. Similarly, the Hanunóo also see all the colors that we see and, when they need to, they adjust their language somewhat. For example, the Hanunóo might say that something is *mabirabiru* to indicate that it is "somewhat mabiru," that is, reddish but lacking the deep darkness that the basic term implies. Or they might call something *mabiru gid* "very mabiru" if it is close to jet black, the color closest to the center of the *mabiru* color group. Thus, clearly the Hanunóo could create more color words if the need arose within their lifestyle. It is also safe to assume that other peoples whose languages currently lack a large number of specific color terms could create them if cultural needs for such terms arose. Indeed, this point is proved by the fact that among Hanunóo men, a hunting color classification has developed based on the need to clearly point out differences in reds and gray—colors that are important in identifying wildlife. Hanunóo women, on the other hand, have developed a more complex vocabulary for shades of blue to distinguish the colors of dyed textiles that have been introduced into their society.

Cultural differences in the richness of semantic domains help us discover what the people of each culture deem to be important in their daily lives. For instance, a language that is rich with emotional descriptors suggests that emotions, feelings, and sensitivities receive much attention. One can also determine which emotions receive the most attention from the language. English, for example, has a variety of terms for self-blame ("shame," "grief," "guilt," and "fear"). Equally true are the words belonging to the semantic domain for emotions implying blaming others ("anger," "resentment," "disgust," and "jealousy"). This concern reveals much about the psychology and the cultural norms of English-speaking people.

Contrasts between the semantic domains of different cultures also help us better understand cultural differences. For instance, our American culture is technologically complex, and we have developed thousands of words for machines and appliances. Many nonindustrialized societies on the other hand, have a much more elaborate terminology than we do for different kinds of relatives. This fact reveals how much more important kinship and family are in the lives of these technologically simple societies.

The study of semantic domains can also reveal much about the changing cultural history of a society. The Great Basin Shoshoni Indians originally practiced a nomadic hunting way of life. Today, many of the Shoshonis survive by cattle ranching like many of their non-Indian neighbors in Nevada, Utah, and Idaho. The Shoshoni language has adapted to these changes. It still contains a great variety of verbs that were useful in the past for easily talking about various kinds of movement that would have been of interest to hunters. For instance, there is a single Shoshoni word that translates "to make a crunching sound by walking on sand," although it is not commonly used any more. On the other hand, Shoshonis have found it necessary to talk about a great number of new tools that now play a role in their lives. They have expanded the native vocabulary accordingly by borrowing many English words. Therefore, by comparing the Shoshoni language of many years ago with the one of today, one might decipher many of the ways in which the Shoshoni lifestyle has changed.

■ References

Conklin, H. C. (1955). Hanunóo color categories. *Southwest Journal of Anthropology, 11*, 339-344.

Nelson, R. K. (1969). *Hunters of the northern ice*. Chicago: University of Chicago Press.

Peoples, J., & Bailey, G. (1991). *Humanity: An introduction to cultural anthropology*. St. Paul, MN: West.

Rosch, E. (1973). On the internal structure of perceptual and semantic categories. In T. Moore (Ed.), *Cognitive development and the acquisition of language*. New York: Academic Press.

■ Discussion Questions

1.   Applying the concept of semantic domain, name the major color categories that exist in English. Choose one color domain and list as many shades or tones of this color that we have terms for. Try this now with an entirely different semantic domain, such as "hats".

2.   Cultures develop specialized vocabularies due to their needs. Choose a particular occupation or profession that is found in Western culture and identify as many specific terms for that specialty as you can (e.g., an auto mechanic).

■ For Further Exploration

1.   Select a group, such as skiers or surfers, with which you are not very familiar. Investigate the vocabulary that sets them apart from other Americans because of their hobby, employment, or lifestyle. Try to discover how the new terms you learn are organized into various semantic domains that are important to the group.

■ For Additional Reading

Berlin, B., & Kay, P. (1969). *Basic color terms: Their universality and evolution*. Berkeley, CA: University of California Press. A cross-cultural, comparative study of color terminology and of how color terms expand as societies evolve.

Was Hunger the Motivation for Aztec Cannibalism?

■ Stimulus Question

Maslow stated that we must meet our basic needs for food, water, and sex before we are able to address our higher-order needs. Would an entire population resort to cannibalism to meet their need for sufficient protein in their diet?

PEOPLE have practiced cannibalism at various times when faced with starvation. The Donner party tragedy—where snowbound pioneers resorted to cannibalism in the Sierra Nevada Mountains in 1846—is a well-known example from American history. But except for the Aztec empire of ancient Mexico, there has never been an entire civilization that accepted cannibalism as a customary practice. What was the Aztec motivation for its society-wide tradition of cannibalism?

Researchers have pointed out that the Aztec practice was partly the culmination of a religious process of human sacrifice and they understood cannibalism in a religious context. Or, the eating of human flesh may have had important, down-to-earth implications for Aztec nutrition, since they lived in an environment that caused periodic protein deficiencies in their diet. Let's look at each of these factors in turn.

First, consider some of the constraints that existed in the Aztec practice of cannibalism. Aztecs did not eat their own people. The bodies of those eaten were typically slaves or prisoners of war, enemies of the Aztec rather than citizens of the empire. Moreover, not everyone was allowed to eat human flesh. Cannibalism was a privilege granted the families of the hereditary aristocracy and commoners who performed well in warfare and captured sacrificial victims to "feed" the Aztec gods. Listen to the words of Aztec students of the Catholic priest, Fray Bernardino de Sahagun:

> Thus was performed the sacrificial slaying of men, when captives and slaves died, who were called "Those who have died for the god." Thus they took [the captive] up [to the pyramid temple] before the devil, [the priests] going holding him by his hands. And he who was known as the arranger [of captives], this one laid him out upon the sacrificial stone.
>
> And when he had laid him upon it four men stretched him out, [grasping] his arms and legs. And already in the hand of the fire priest lay the [sacrificial] knife, with which he was to slash open the breast of the ceremonially bathed [captive].
>
> And then, when he had split open his breast, he at once seized his heart. And he whose breast he laid open was quite alive. And when [the priest] had seized his heart, he dedicated it to the sun.
>
> Thus was done the eating [of sacrificial victim's blood by the gods': When [the priests] had cut open a slave's or a captive's breast, then [the owner of the victim] took his blood in a vessel and, perchance, cast a paper into the vessel, which drew up the blood.
>
> Then he took [the blood] in the vessel and placed upon the lips of all [the images of] the devils the blood of him who had died for the gods. (Anderson & Dibble, 1951, pp. 184-185)

After the gods dined on the heart and blood of sacrificial victims, the bodies became food for the Aztec people.

Ortiz de Montellano (1978) believes that it was religion that motivated the Aztec to eat human flesh. In the minds of the Aztec, they were participating in a kind of Holy Commmunion with their gods when they shared the food that they also offered their gods. Indeed, according to Ortiz de Montellano, the greatest motive to practice sacrifice and cannibalism had to be religious. The Aztec believed they could avoid the end of the world only by sacrificing victims to feed the gods, especially the Sun God, who carried the sun across the sky each day. So Aztecs who performed bravely in battle and brought home captives for sacrifice were honored with high social status.

According to Aztec theology, the gods rewarded sacrificial victims with a glorious afterlife. Just as those who captured and offered sacrifice were rewarded on earth with high standing, sacrificial victims became minor gods in the next world. They went to dwell with the god who fed upon them and became minor gods themselves. Ortiz de Montellano argues that this willingness to cooperate in their own deaths was evidence that religion was the real foundation for people's motives in Aztec sacrifice and cannibalism.

When people ate the bodies of those who died as sacrifices, they believed they were eating the flesh of a god. So eating their flesh was considered a privilege given from heaven to the deserving, the high-ranking 25% of the Aztec population who were numbered among the nobility. Seventy-five percent of the Aztec were never permitted to practice cannibalism at all.

Ortiz de Montellano argues that there was no real need for a protein supplement in the Aztec diet, even during times of famine. He also contends that the amount of human flesh eaten was not a significant contribution to the diet of these people. For instance, Garn and Block (1970) demonstrated that the carefully butchered body of a 110-pound man is not likely to have yielded more than 66 pounds of edible muscle. This amount of meat would contain only about 9.9 pounds of protein for domestic consumption. Taking into account the weekly amount of protein needs for an average person, they concluded that one sacrificial victim would have served 60 people skimpily. It is clear, then, that human flesh was never the staple food of the Aztec diet. Yet, the amount of human flesh was certainly not insignificant either. Some scholars however, have estimated that the Aztec people sacrificed and ate a number of victims that might have equaled 1% of their own population each year! Michael Harner (1977) analyzed the nutritional impact of such a large amount of meat on the Aztec society and, along with a number of other anthropologists, believes that more than just religious obligation was at the root of the Aztec food customs. In Harner's view the Aztec acceptance of cannibalism was part of the society's adjustment to an environment in which protein scarcity was an important fact of life. Early Mexican hunters had caused the extinction of all the native herbivores that were suitable for domestication as foods. Similarly, wild meat foods were no longer readily available by Aztec times. For instance, the deer was almost extinct (Vaillant, 1966, p. 142). For Harner, then, human sacrifice filled a natural dietary need for Aztec civilization. Harner argues that "in the guise of satisfying gods, the priests actually were authorizing a hungry population to go forth and seize humans destined for consumption" (Harner, 1977, p. 130).

Those who support Harner's hypothesis of dietary motivation for Aztec cannibalism have enlarged upon his original position, noting that those who argue for a primarily religious motivation have not really explained why a society would practice cannibalism—they have merely described the context in which cannibalism occurred. After all, why people would be motivated to practice a religion that encourages human sacrifice and cannibalism is no less a mystery than why they would adopt cannibalism in the first place. "Explaining" Aztec cannibalism by saying it was religiously motivated therefore leaves us with the same mystery we started with.

It has been suggested that advocates of the "religious motivation" viewpoint have been naive in their confusion of Aztec religious *ideals* with Aztec *behavior*. Consider the following: It is certainly true that the human sacrifices that preceded cannibalistic feasts were religious affairs. They were performed at the tops of pyramids on which stood the temples of the Aztec gods, and the hearts and blood of the sacrificial victims were offered to those gods. It is also true that the religious beliefs of the Aztec and their neighbors included the consoling promise that those who were sacrificed to feed the gods would become minor gods themselves. Did sacrificial victims really march happily up the steps of pyramids to their deaths because of such promises? If not, and they were not the willing victims Ortiz de Montellano describes, then the "religion as motivation" argument loses much of its strength.

Accounts of Aztec human sacrifice and of the participants' actual behavior—a more realistic basis to judge their real motivations—paint a very different picture from the one drawn by Ortiz de Montellano. The Franciscan priest Motolinia (1951) wrote in the early 1500s:

> Let no one think that any of those who were sacrificed by being slain and having their hearts torn out or being killed in any other way, suffered death voluntarily and not by force. They had to submit to it, feeling great grief over their death and enduring frightful pain. (p. 116)

And in the *Florentine Codex*, it is recorded:

> When the masters of the captives took their slaves to the temple where they were to slay them, they took them by the hair. And when they took them up the steps of the pyramid, some of the captives swooned, and their masters pulled them up and dragged them by the hair to the sacrificial stone where they were to die. (Anderson & Dibble, 1951, p. 3)

Harris (1985), in expanding Harner's claim that the Aztec were motivated by dietary needs to practice cannibalism, notes that the basic problem that ceremonial cannibalism addressed was not a need to provide meat for every citizen but to supplement the diet of certain members of the Aztec population during the most critical times of protein shortage. The Aztec usually met their protein needs not with meat but with plant crops that provided the amino acids our bodies need to build its own protein. This approach was not fully successful during the times of periodic drought in the high Mexican desert, and the lack of a meat industry opened the door to cannibalism.

Only the aristocracy could practice cannibalism, but admission to the aristocracy was fairly liberal. Any commoner who joined the military and brought home sacrificial victims was elevated to its ranks and allowed to feed his family on the meat he had captured. Thus, unlike the commoners of France in Marie Antoinette's day, the most militant among the hungry masses had a very personal motive for supporting the Aztec government. After all, patriotism brought them meat–exactly what their diet lacked. The soldiers who went out to do battle might well have spoken of their efforts in religious terms, but by feeding their gods they were also feeding their families. So Aztec human sacrifice supplemented the diets of those most likely to rebel against the aristocracy in harsh times. It was a way of inspiring loyalty rather than unrest in times of dietary stress. Cannibalism rewarded those who gave allegiance to Aztec politics and religion in a very practical way. It helped them survive—not by feeding everyone but by buying the loyalty of those most likely or capable of rebelling.

■ References

Anderson, A. J. O., & Dibble, C. E. (1951). *Florentine Codex: General history of the things of New Spain. Book 2–The ceremonies.* Santa Fe, NM: The School of American Research and The University of Utah.

Garn, S. M., & Block, W. D. (1970). The limited nutritional value of cannibalism. *American Anthropologist, 72,* 106.

Harner, M. (1977). The ecological basis of Aztec cannibalism. *American Ethnologist, 4,* 117-135.

Harris, M. (1985). *Good to eat: Riddles of food and culture.* New York: Simon & Schuster.

Motolinia, T. (1951). *Motolinia's history of the Indians of New Spain* (F. B. Steck, Trans.). Washington, D.C.: Academy of American Franciscan History.

Ortiz de Montellano, B. R. (1978). Aztec cannibalism: An ecological necessity? *Science, 200,* 611-617.

Vaillant, C. G. (1966). *Aztecs of Mexico: The rise and fall of the Aztec nation* (rev. ed. by S. B. Valliant). Harmondsworth, Middlesex, England: Penguin Books.

■ Discussion Questions

1.   Is there evidence that the Aztecs had a dietary need for protein that normal food sources could not meet?

2.   Why might cannibalism make sense in terms of what "human" consumption would add to the typical Aztec diet?

3.   What argument is advanced for the theory that cannibalism was most likely motivated by religious beliefs?

■ For Further Exploration

1.   What historical and current examples demonstrate a religious zeal or commitment among Western societies that is similar to that of the Aztecs?
2.   List behaviors that are generally not acceptable in our culture. Under what circumstances, or with what motivation, might you consider engaging in them?

■ For Additional Reading

Harris, M. (1985). *Good to eat: Riddles of food and culture*. New York: Simon & Schuster. This fascinating look at food preferences and food taboos in a variety of the world's cultures covers cannibalism, the American love affair with beef, Islamic and Jewish rejection of the pig, the Hindu sacred cow, and a number of other equally interesting examples of the motivation to eat or not to eat.

Aggression:
The Nonviolent Semai

■ Stimulus Questions

Can culture order the lives of people so that aggression is an unusual aspect of their behavior? If so, under what conditions might ordinarily nonviolent people act aggressively?

THE DEBATE about the causes of human aggression has raged since time immemorial. Are humans innately aggressive, or is aggression a learned phenomenon? We humans are clearly *capable* of being rather violent at times. But this should not be confused with the claim made by some that we have an innate *tendency* to be aggressive. Anthropologists have studied societies in which warfare is nonexistent and in which interpersonal violence is a rare occurrence. One such society is a Malaysian group called the Semai.

The Semai are farming people in central West Malaysia whose unaggressive nature and customs were described by Dentan (1968). They had no need for police, judges, or jails. Their government was based on cooperation within the village, with no one empowered to enforce rules. The Semai simply assumed cooperation to be normal and conceived of themselves as nonviolent. According to Dentan, their nonviolent self-image "is not merely an ideal to strive for. The Semai do not say, 'Anger is bad.' They say, 'We do not get angry,' and an obviously angry man will flatly deny his anger. The Semai do not say, 'It is forbidden to hit people.' They say, 'We do not hit people'" (pp. 55-56).

The Semai contrast themselves with outsiders in regard to their treatment of children. Other people, according to the Semai, hit their children, but the Semai do not. According to the Semai, you should never hit a child. After all, "How would you feel if it died?" they ask (Dentan, p. 58). According to Dentan, the Semai almost never hit their children. Physical aggression among adults is also rare. Dentan says, "Some idea of the horror that physical violence implies in Semai is revealed by the fact that when east Semai are talking Malay they translate their word for 'hit' as 'kill'" (p. 58).

True, Semai individuals sometimes violate their expectations of nonviolence, but this is rare. For instance, Dentan found that murder was almost unthinkable to the Semai. People claimed that there were no penalties for murder, because "it never happens, in the olden days or today" (p. 58). Indeed, Dentan could find no instance of murder, attempted murder, or maiming among the Semai from 1956 through 1968. He summarized the role of violence among the Semai this way:

> In brief, little violence occurs within Semai society. Violence, in fact, seems to terrify the Semai. A Semai does not meet force with force, but with passivity or flight. Yet, he has no institutionalized way of preventing violence—no social controls, no police or courts. Somehow a Semai learns automatically always to keep tight rein over his aggressive impulses. Given the weakness of external controls, the Semai need internal ones. (p. 59)

The Semai have no authority figures in their society. There are no "headmen" such as those in the rest of Malaysia who have authority to give orders. Trying to make others do something they do not want to do is unacceptable behavior. Even parents do not have authority to force their will on their children, and the Semai have no word for "adult" in their language. If a child does not want to do what its parents ask it to do, the parents let it follow its own inclinations. How then do the Semai socialize their children into a life in which they think of themselves as nonviolent—and generally behave unaggressively toward others?

The Semai do not believe that they actively teach their children. Rather, they believe that children simply learn by themselves. It is their view that if a child is unready or unwilling to learn, coercion will not be effective. Indeed, any coercion is taboo. The actual Semai word for "taboo" is *punang*, which means behavior that is unacceptable because it makes someone else unhappy and, therefore, accident prone. Again, that the Semai wish not to be the cause of harm to others is at the bottom of their child-rearing practices.

Paradoxically, letting Semai children have their own way doesn't open the door to aggression on their part, probably because they have no aggressive (or coercive) role models.

Many Semai believe that children are inherently "naughty," however, and to teach their children to refrain from improper behavior, they use fear tactics. They may shout at a child and even threaten to hit it, although, according to Dentan, "the blow freezes inches away from its target, and the worst the child usually gets is a tap" (p. 60). It is this inhibiting of aggression that the child models. In one game:

> [C]hildren of both sexes from two- to ten-year-olds flail away wildly at each other with long sticks, assuming dramatically aggressive postures. Yet the sticks always freeze inches away from the target, and although it seems inevitable that someone will be hit by mistake, no one ever is. (p. 59)

This pattern of inhibited aggression shows up in other forms of play as well. For instance, in wrestling, children will throw their opponents almost, but not quite, to the ground.

Parents also try to instill fear by telling a child to be afraid when the child is behaving improperly. For instance, the Semai encourage their children to fear nonSemai: "The Pale People have come to stick you with hypodermics. . . . Fear! Fear! They are going to eat you! Fear! Fear!" (p. 60). In thunderstorms, adults also cry "Fear!" and encourage children to cover their eyes and ears. Later, the same word, "Fear!" will be yelled at a child who is becoming noisy or who is about to lose self-control.

Although the Semai do not punish aggression in their children, they have a low tolerance for it. They expect their children to conform to the Semai self-image of nonviolence, and they communicate this expectation by how they react when children show aggression. According to Dentan:

> Children become aware of this expectation as it is manifested both in subtle daily ways and in the open shock of adults when a child loses its temper. In the latter case, an adult immediately snatches up the angry child and carries it off wailing to its house. This abrupt intervention is probably all the more frightening because adults usually are indifferent to children's activities. (p. 60)

It's hardly surprising that by the time Semai are adults, their attitude toward the very thought of violence is one of horror. Does this mean that no Semai ever engages in aggression? By no means. The Semai are much less violent than Americans, but they do violate their own rules occasionally, just as we do. According to Robarchek and Dentan (1987), "Dentan has seen an east Semai man beat a dog that stole food from his baby, for instance, and another throw a frog against a tree to kill it rather than have to carry it home to eat" (p. 362). The Semai also cook birds and other small animals alive but they do not think of this as aggression, since they do not anthropomorphize animals the way Euro-Americans do. According to Robarchek and Dentan, "For them, such actions seem no more emotionally charged than killing a mosquito, scarcely as overwhelming as the eruption of repressed emotions would be in Freudian theory" (p. 362).

During the Communist insurgency of the early 1950s, the Semai had their first taste of warfare when the British recruited troops from among them. Initially, the Semai recruits did not seem to comprehend the role they were expected to play. According to Dentan, many Semai recruits did not realize that soldiers kill people: "When I suggested to one east Semai recruit that killing was a soldier's job, he laughed at my ignorance and explained, 'No, we don't kill people, brother, we just tend weeds and cut grass.' Apparently, he had up to that point done nothing but grounds duty" (p. 58).

Nevertheless, although many who knew the Semai did not expect them to make good soldiers, the Semai recruits sometimes outperformed all expectations. In Dentan's words:

> A typical veteran's story runs like this. "We killed, killed, killed. The Malays would stop and go through people's pockets and take their watches and money. We did not think of watches or money. We thought only of killing. Wah, truly we were drunk with blood." One man even told how he had drunk the blood of a man he had killed. (pp. 58-59)

It appears that the Semai were certainly capable of extremes of violence when they were removed from their normal cultural environment. The Semai veterans were unable to account for their own extreme behavior and, on returning home, reverted to their former gentle and timid style of life. In spite of their military experience, their traditional nonviolent self-image remained intact when they returned to civilian life.

A number of writers have portrayed the Semai "blood-drunkenness" as an outburst of aggression that Semai culture had kept bottled up. These writers have used the Semai as evidence for an innate aggressiveness in humans (Eible-Eibesfeld, 1978; Konner, 1982; Paul, 1978; Wilson, 1978). However, Robarchek and Dentan believe that this overstates the facts. In their opinion, the drastic change in some Semai is explainable by circumstances that made it easier for them to become violent when their military situation encouraged them to do so. Most Semai in the military did not give themselves over to extremes of violence. For instance, over a twenty-year period, the original Semai unit of 300 to 400 soldiers killed an average of only one person per year. Thus, the typical Semai soldier was not dramatically violent.

Robarchek and Dentan also point out that many of the Semai who were involved in violence had been previously affected by terrorists who had murdered a number of influential Semai. The British had bombed and strafed Semai villages, driving the people into the rain forests. They then told the Semai that it had been the Communist insurgents who had harmed them. In the opinion of Robarchek and Dentan, the violent outburst of a few Semai soldiers simply proves that we all have the capacity for violence even if nonviolence is our cultural and personal ideal. The violent Semai soldiers were simply "people with little or no prior experience in either committing or dealing with violence, transplanted from an egalitarian, peaceful society into one that taught and rewarded killing, where they were trained in military behavior, including how to kill" (p. 361). In the "heat, fear, and excitement of a sudden firefight" they did what they had been trained to do against enemies they believed had harmed and killed their own neighbors and friends.

Robarchek and Dentan also argue that the Semai concept of "blood drunkenness" has been misunderstood, because the English phrase has very different connotations than the original Semai term from which it is translated, *buul bhiib*. The "drunkenness" of *buul bhiib* does not have the connotation of "pleasurable wooziness and loss of restraint that Americans associate with being drunk, but an 'intoxication' which disorients and nauseates" (p. 360). Semai veterans who killed and then described themselves as "blood drunk" were not saying that they had gone berserk with a lust to kill. Quite the contrary, they meant that they had felt "an acute state of nausea, fear, disorientation, and disgust which the sight of human blood evokes among the Semai" (p. 361).

The Semai, then, seem to tell us that although all humans may be violent under the right circumstances, people can also be socialized to inhibit aggression in their daily lives. It is even possible for people who are socialized to live nonviolently to incorporate an image of nonviolence into their self-image. They might still behave aggressively when so encouraged by special circumstances, but they will probably be bewildered and even disgusted by their own behavior and will return to their nonviolent lifestyle as soon as circumstances permit.

■ References

Dentan, R. K. (1968). *The Semai: A nonviolent people of Malaya*. New York: Holt, Rinehart & Winston.

Eible-Eibesfeld, I. (1978). *The biology of peace and war*. New York: Viking Press.

Konner, M. (1982). *The tangled wing: Biological constraints on the human spirit*. New York: Holt, Rinehart & Winston.

Paul, R. (1978). Instinctive aggression in man: The Semai case. *Journal of Psychological Anthropology, 1*, 65-79.

Robarchek, C. A., & Dentan, R. K. (1987). Blood drunkenness and the bloodthirsty Semai: Unmaking another anthropological myth. *American Anthropologist, 89*, 356-365.

Wilson, E. O. (1978). *On human nature*. Cambridge, MA: Harvard University Press.

■ Discussion Questions

1.   How did Dentan account for the nonviolence of the Semai?

2.   How do Robarchek and Dentan explain the violent behavior of some Semai in the military?

3.   Explain why the English phrase, "blood-drunkenness" is a poor translation of the Semai term, *buul bhiib*. What misunderstanding has this translation led to?

■ For Further Exploration

1.   Debate the question, "Is it possible to design a research study that would conclusively demonstrate that human beings are innately aggressive or nonaggressive?" What are the methodological issues involved? Is it possible to design a study that distinguishes between a capacity for violence and a natural tendency for aggression?

■ For Additional Reading

Chagnon, N. A. (1968). *Yánomamo: The fierce people*. New York: Holt, Rinehart & Winston. A description of a Venezuelan/Brazilian tribal society in which almost one in four men died violently each generation.

Otterbein, K. F. (1970). *The evolution of war*. New Haven, CT: Human Resource Area Files. Traces the development of group conflict from the simplest to the most complex societies.

Vayda, A. P. (1976). *War in ecological perspective*. New York: Plenum. Examines the role of the environment in the forms of warfare in traditional societies.

Individualism vs. Collectivism: Differences Between Chinese and American Value Orientations

■ Stimulus Question

Value orientations may help explain behavioral differences between groups of people. How do our societal values influence what we believe and how we act toward other people, including our friends and family?

RUGGED INDIVIDUALISM, or the spirit of self-reliance, can be readily identified as a value highly promoted in our society. Together with a strong value placed on competitiveness, standing on one's own two feet is a value orientation most middle-class American children learn early in life. In this society, we can see many examples of a strong socialization process for children to become independent, self-sufficient persons. As cultural psychologists, however, we need to be aware that this "John Wayneism" is neither found nor promoted in all cultures.

On the other side of this values "coin" are those societies or cultures that can be described as having the "collectivism" orientation. Hsu (1981) defines this value orientation as (a) being more concerned with others, (b) considering the implications for others of one's decisions, and (c) sharing of material resources. Groups demonstrating a collectivistic point of view are thought of as more socially oriented. In societies with a higher emphasis on the social group, individuals are expected to show less autonomy and develop a more conforming, group-welfare orientation. The collectivist orientation emphasizes that group achievement is more important than individual achievement and believes in a greater distribution of rewards to all in-group members regardless of actual individual accomplishments. This difference is illustrated by Robert Whiting's (1979) discussion of the difficulties that American baseball players have experienced adjusting to playing on Japanese teams, where unity and team play is rewarded more than striving to be an individual hero. Where Americans speak of "doing your own thing," the Japanese use the proverb, "The nail that sticks up shall be hammered down." Whiting cites the example of baseball player John Miller, who in 1972 was released for misconduct. In addition to such problems as frequently showing up five or ten minutes late for practice without apologizing for keeping his teammates waiting, he committed the unpardonable sin of blowing off steam when he was removed for a pinch hitter by yelling, "I don't care if this team wins or not." In spite of an apology and although he finished the year as his team's leader in home runs, he was released when the season ended. Another American, a better team player, was kept even though he batted only .190.

This orientation has also been described as an outcome for a society that places a strong emphasis on the extended family—as with the Chinese—and instills the notion that a person belongs to a unit larger than himself or herself (Gabrenya, Latane, & Wang, 1983). Finally, Domino and Hannah (1987) state the Chinese value system is qualitatively different from that found in American culture. One particular difference concerns the individualism-collectivism dimension. The greater social orientation of the Chinese places more emphasis on public shame as an arbiter of behavior. The effect of this is to increase the importance of teamwork and to minimize the possibility of individuals acting as agents for themselves.

In a study by Domino and Hannah (1987) the value orientations of Chinese and American children (ages 11 to 13) were analyzed by means of a story completion technique. Children from each culture were given a number of story plots to which they responded. For instance, the researchers stated, "As Peter and Frank walk to school, Frank throws Peter's cap into a tree, and retrieval is difficult." Or, "John and Bill are playing ball and break a neighbor's window, but no one sees them do it." From this beginning children explained what then happened to the characters by way of their own story. Domino and Hannah analyzed over 700 stories for content themes generated by the 80 Chinese children from Beijing and the 80 American children from Los Angeles. Their results confirmed the expected individualistic-collectivistic differences between children from these two cultures. Specifically, in their stories, Chinese children emphasized the greater social interest orientation which they, as a group, have been characterized as displaying. Significantly more Chinese children said, in one way or another, that the group is their standard for the acceptance or rejection of a behavior. Public shame, which would result in family dishonor or embarrassment, comes through in Chinese stories but never in the stories offered by the American children. Furthermore, at an early age, group unity is already a valuable goal which Chinese children have acquired through social-ization. Deviant behavior brings shame not only onto the individual but also onto the entire group.

Finally, as another puzzle piece we can use to better understand the development of the collectivist perspective, there is a greater importance placed on respecting authority by the Chinese. Just as others have noted, Domino and Hannah found that Chinese children emphasized good behavior, cooperation, and obedience. In conclusion, the self-reliant, individualistic American way seen in stories told by 11 to 13 year old American children was in opposition to the concern of the Chinese for the approval of others and the welfare of the group.

To demonstrate further the collectivist orientation, we can look to the anthropology literature which describes a Chinese concept of *t'ung-yang-hsi*. Literally translated, this term means "daughter-in-law raised from childhood" (Wolf, 1968). So great was the Chinese concern for harmony within the family, one of the important aspects of collectivism, that some families chose to socialize their own daughters-in-law by taking them into the household at a very young age. These girls were brought up as if they were a daughter in that home, but at the appropriate age they would marry one of the sons in that family.

As recently as the 1950s, *t'ung-yang-hsi* was reportedly practiced extensively throughout South China and Taiwan. Historically, very strong parents ruled over the Chinese extended family. This form of marriage practice was intended to reduce some of the friction which would arise between the mother and her daughter-in-law. Since this clash between mother-in-law and daughter-in-law was quite predictable (as evidenced by what happened when a girl from another family married and took up residence in her husband's household), the practice of bringing into the family the son's bride-to-be years before the actual marriage was seen as having some distinct advantages. By raising the "adopted" female child as a daughter, a different kind of loyalty developed in her than in a daughter-in-law, raised by her own biological parents, who married into the family much later. Under these circumstances, the *t'ung-yang-hsi* was first of all a daughter and only later a daughter-in-law and wife. Her first allegiance was owed to her "parents." Allegiance to her husband came second.

The Chinese family is best understood from a collectivistic point of view. It is nothing like the independent, nuclear family found in Western cultures. A son was expected to be loyal and attentive to his mother. As a new daughter-in-law came into her husband's family, jealousy created the inevitable problems between the son's mother and his new wife. A *t'ung-yang-hsi*, as described above, experienced neither jealousy nor animosity toward her mother-in-law because of her husband's attentiveness to his mother. Rarely would she be accused of turning her husband against her new mother-in-law. If anything, daughter-in-law and mother-in-law acted as allies against the husband/son. Conflict was more likely to occur between husband and wife than between generations living in the same household.

Within the collectivistic mentality, the fear of losing one's son was great enough to devise a system such as the *t'ung-yang-hsi* which had the effect of preserving harmony within the family. Although certain benefits associated with marrying outside the family were lost, the family's benefits from having a *t'ung-yang hsi* outweighed these losses, as evidenced by the number of families, rich and poor, practicing this form of marriage.

Finally, the concept of "social loafing" may be useful in demonstrating collectivism vs. individualism differences seen among different cultures. Social loafing describes the following phenomenon: individuals exert less of an effort on a task when they are performing or working as a group than if they are doing the same task by themselves. This phenomenon has been explained as what will happen if people do not see their efforts making a unique contribution. If people's efforts blend, individual recognition and rewards are less likely. Gabrenya, Wang, and Latane (1985) were interested in whether or not this phenomenon was transcultural. Specifically, would Chinese students, coming from a collectivistic-type society, also demonstrate the social loafing generally found to be characteristic of Americans? They found that social loafing was *not* a universal phenomenon. They conclude that because of stronger group-oriented values, the Chinese students show just the opposite tendency, what they termed "social striving". On group performance tasks, Chinese students exerted a greater effort than did Americans.

Once a value has been internalized by a person, it acts as a standard or guide for his or her behavior. Thus, if group cohesiveness is important, we would expect to see greater efforts on the part of individuals for their group. The group welfare and achievements become the primary goal.

■ References

Domino, G., & Hannah, M.T. (1987). A comparative analysis of social values of Chinese and American children. *Journal of Cross-Cultural Psychology, 18,* 58-77.

Gabrenya, W.K., Latane, B., & Wang, Y. (1983). Social loafing in cross-cultural perspective: Chinese on Taiwan. *Journal of Cross-Cultural Psychology, 14,* 368-384.

Gabrenya, W.K., Wang, Y., & Latane, B. (1985). Social loafing on an optimizing task: Cross-cultural differences among Chinese and Americans. *Journal of Cross-Cultural Psychology, 16,* 223-242.

Hsu, F.L.K. (1981). *Americans and Chinese: Two ways of life.* Honolulu: University of Hawaii Press.

Whiting, R. (1979, September 24). You've gotta have 'Wa'. *Sports Illustrated,* pp. 60-71.

Wolf, A.P. (1968). Adopt a daughter-in-law, marry a sister: A Chinese solution to the problem of the incest taboo. *American Anthropologist, 70,* 864-874.

■ Discussion Questions

1.   Identify at least three concepts which distinguish the collectivistic from the individualistic type of thinking or point of view.

2.   From a research perspective, what is the advantage of collecting "value" data using a technique like the one employed by Domino and Hannah?

3.   Why can the concept of *t'ung-yang-hsi* be used to exemplify the collectivistic orientation? As Chinese society continues to change will we see this practice continuing to exist? Explain.

4.   Discuss why a more collectivistic orientation would probably *not* become accepted as the norm in a society such as ours. What values do we have which would not be compatible with collectivism?

A Frown Is a Frown Is a Frown: Facial Expressions Around the World

■ Stimulus Question

Is a smile or a frown interpreted the same way in every society?

ACCORDING to a popular quote of Gertrude Stein, "Rose is a rose is a rose." Can the same thing be said of emotional expressions? Would a simple smile, regardless of the culture in which it is found, always indicate a state of happiness? Would surprise be shown with the same facial expression everywhere? Evidence does exist to support the hypothesis that numerous facial expressions are universal.

In a 1969 study by Ekman, subjects from seven different Western and non-Western cultures showed no significant differences in the way they matched up words describing emotion with facial expressions. However, such a study can be criticized because the two non-Western, preliterate societies in the study had extensive prior contact with Western cultures. Perhaps the non-Western groups had learned the foreign facial conventions and recognized them because of this exposure.

Aware of this problem, Ekman later attempted to discover if people with minimal contact with Western societies would perform the same way. So he located a very isolated group of people called the Fore who lived in the Southeast Highlands of Papua, New Guinea, and had had very little contact with foreigners (Ekman & Friesen, 1971; Ekman,

1973, pp. 169-176). Ekman tested 3% of the entire Fore population—189 adults and 130 children—to see how they recognized various facial expressions of emotion. He also tested a second group, using individuals who had experienced significant contact with the West. Ekman's methodology was to tell stories in which a person experienced happiness, sadness, anger, surprise, disgust, or fear, then display three photos of people's faces, only one of which correctly illustrated the emotion of the person in the story. He paired various combinations of correct and incorrect photos, and included some groupings of photos with facial expressions that were difficult to discriminate among. For example, when sadness was expressed in the story, the researchers showed people a photo of a sad expression along with photos representing anger and disgust.

Ekman found no significant differences between males and females in their ability to judge emotional expression. Fore women had had even less contact with Westerners than Fore men. So the similarity of women's and men's judgments lent support to the idea that there are universal ways of showing emotions with facial expressions.

When the responses of all Fore adults were considered as a group, they identified every emotion except fear and surprise at a statistically significant level. Analysis of the more Westernized sample revealed identical results. Again, only discriminating between fear and surprise gave respondents problems. There were no significant differences between more Westernized and less Westernized adults. When children were tested for their ability to recognize facial expressions appropriate for an emotional story, older children were no better at this task than were younger children. Similar work carried out among the Grand Valley Dani of West Irian, New Guinea, by Karl and Eleanor Heider (reported in Ekman, 1973, pp. 210-214) yielded the same results.

Ekman (1972, pp. 239-260; 1973, pp. 214-228) also compared two industrialized groups, Japanese and Americans, in a different kind of study on how emotion is facially expressed. Members of both groups were filmed while they viewed two different motion pictures. One of the movies that they watched was a film of eye surgery; the other was a nonstressful film. Films of their facial expressions were then rated for the type of emotion exhibited. Another group of Japanese and American subjects were also rated on their abilities to recognize when the first group was viewing the stressful versus nonstressful films. Some of the original subjects were alone when they were filmed, others were filmed in the presence of another person.

The results showed that for subjects who were filmed alone, there were no differences between the facial expressions of Japanese and

Americans. There were also no differences between Japanese and Americans in their abilities to recognize when members of their own group or the other group were watching the stressful film. These results seem to confirm the that both the expression of various emotions and the ability to recognize emotions in facial expression is a human universal. However, this interesting study did show important differences between Japanese and American subjects in facial reactions to films *for those subjects who were filmed in the presence of other people*. Japanese subjects in this case were significantly less likely to show their distress at viewing the eye-surgery films than were the Americans. These Japanese also smiled more frequently than the Americans. Thus, Japanese culture apparently had a strong impact in causing Japanese subjects to inhibit their expression of emotion—and to put on a more positive front—when they were not alone.

We can conclude that although emotions are universally expressed through the same facial behaviors, culture may play an important role in determining when it is acceptable to socially display an emotion. Thus, children and adults alike, from the jungles of New Guinea to urban America, express similar emotions with the same type of facial expressions. Cultures, however, may vary in their rules about the appropriateness of showing certain emotional responses in particular situations.

■ References

Ekman, P., & Friesen, W.V. (1971). Constants across cultures in the face and emotion. *Journal of Personality and Social Psychology*, *17*, 124-129.

Ekman, P. (1972). Universals and cultural differences in facial expressions of emotion. In J. K. Cole (Ed.), *Nebraska symposium on motivation 1971*. (pp. 207-283). Lincoln, NE: University of Nebraska Press.

Ekman, P. (1973). Cross-cultural studies of facial expression. In P. Ekman (Ed.), *Darwin and facial expression: A century of research in review*. (pp. 169-222). New York: Academic Press.

■ Discussion Questions

1. What evidence is there to support a universal theory of emotional expression?

2. Why is cross-cultural psychological research so difficult to conduct? Can you think of other psychological variables that would also be difficult to measure within or between cultures?

3.   Ekman states that the two emotions most difficult to discriminate between were "fear" and "surprise." What explanation can you suggest for this?

■ For Further Exploration

1.   Discuss difficulties that language differences might pose in research on the expression and recognition of various emotions in different cultures?

■ For Additional Reading

Izard, C. E. (1971). *The face of emotion*. New York: Appleton-Century-Crofts. A study of the expression of emotion by a researcher whose independent work paralleled that of Ekman.

Witch-Fear Among the Aivilik Eskimo

■ Stimulus Question

What conditions could cause a generalized fear of witchcraft in an entire population?

FEAR is what you feel when you believe you do not have enough power to remain safe from the undesired effects of some specific problem (Kemper, 1978). In many of the world's cultures, religious beliefs support the fear of witchcraft, and victims truly believe that their misfortunes are the result of the evil powers of a witch. The behaviors of people who believe themselves to have been bewitched appear similar to the symptoms of *generalized anxiety disorder*. Persons suffering from this disorder have unrealistic expectations, excessive worry, and fantasies associated with a heightened level of anxiety. The degree of anxiety increases with the severity and perceived likelihood of anticipated harm. Fear of dying is not uncommon.

Carpenter (1953) has described the changing perceptions of magic and witchcraft among the Aivilik Eskimo, a small group of 120 people from Southhampton Island north of Hudson Bay, who at one time depended on hunting as their primary means of subsistence in the harsh Arctic environment. Until very recently, "white magic"—magic used for moral purposes—was an important ingredient in Aivilik life. Magical formulas existed for many positive purposes, such as curing illness or luring game. The importance of white magic waned after European contact brought disaster to the Aivilik way of life, and the belief in witchcraft, the evil use of supernatural power to harm other people, grew stronger as an explanation for misfortunes such as newly introduced diseases. These hunting people worried a lot about witchcraft, suffering considerable tension and anxiety as a result. By 1950, witch-fear was pervasive in this society.

Although the Aivilik understood that a misfortune might have a natural explanation such as bacteria or faulty ammunition in a rusty gun, they invariably cited witchcraft as the explanation of why that particular misfortune happened to a particular individual at a particular time. For example, during a hunting expedition, a hunter's shot accidentally wounded another Aivilik man. Various conditions could easily have explained how the misfortune happened: The boat was overcrowded, and the hunter was too excited, perhaps even careless. However, the fact that this accident should have happened unpredictably to that particular victim at that precise moment was believed to be the result of witchcraft. Witchcraft links an individual to a specific unfortunate event, whatever the natural, mundane causes of that event might be. The existential questions of "Why me?" or "Why now?" always call for transcendent or spiritual answers, such as "bad luck," "God's will," "fate," or "witchcraft." In this respect the Aivilik are no different from any other people who wonder not just how something bad happens but also why it happens, especially when it happens to good or innocent people. The Aivilik differ from most others in attributing the cause of misfortune to powerful *evil* forces at work. Whereas alternative answers to such questions offer solace and help us rise above misfortune, the witchcraft answer inspires continuing anxiety. After all, where witches are continually at work, one must be continually on guard. The Aivilik experience the ongoing anxiety of wondering who are the witches who caused the misfortune? When and where will they strike next? How can we avoid or fight back against them? It is this aspect of witchcraft belief that is reminiscent of anxiety disorders.

What led the Aivilik culture down a path that stimulated so much anxiety in life? The increasing strength of the Aivilik belief in witchcraft corresponded to the waning of Aivilik religious values based on traditional white magic, which was no longer a match for a quickly changing world. Contact with European civilization had brought an increase in deadly diseases, decimation of their game herds, and conflicts with other hostile Eskimo groups. White magic could not cure these diseases, and magic seemed less able to insure successful hunting as the game grew scarce. In its place, witchcraft offered at least an explanation for the evils and misfortunes that happened with increasing frequency as their society was changed by European immigration. Witchcraft was both consistent with Aivilik culture and socially relevant to these people.

The Aivilik had traditionally explained natural death by witchcraft. It is easy to understand someone's death in natural terms when that person was murdered or killed by an animal. But natural causes are less obvious when someone stops living due to unseen causes such as a heart attack, or stroke. An example of death by natural causes and the role of witchcraft is the case of an Aivilik couple, Kainuk and Mikkoshark, who had had a long, unpleasant marriage. People believed that Kainuk bewitched his wife and that this ultimately caused her death. Before dying, however, Mikkoshark concluded that Kainuk had bewitched her and publicly stated that her ghost would take care of him after her death. Carpenter (1953) gives the following account:

> Following his wife's death, Kainuk's behavior became so unbalanced that there was talk of doing away with him. He became convinced that the goddess Sumna was irrevocably determined to betray him at every turn in his life and to torture him eternally in the next. He was visited by apocalyptic visions; mind-freezing apparitions of his wife shrieked in his ears. On several occasions, mistaking his daughter for his wife's ghost, he attacked her with rocks and edged weapons. Everyone expected his wife's spirit to take him quickly, but then he seemed to recover and for the better part of one day was calm and restful. The next morning he did not awaken from his sleep, and all knew that his wife at last had won. (p. 196)

In a similar case, Santainna, an Aivilik hunter, became ill because he believed his deceased wife had bewitched him. His wife had developed tuberculosis and went off to a sanatorium. However, she believed that it was her husband who caused this to happen to her so that he could take a younger wife. Santainna's behavior with other women while his wife was in the sanatorium only reinforced her suspicions. When Santainna's wife died, he became "paralyzed with fear" (p. 198). He was quite certain that her ghost would return to retaliate and the Aivilik believed a person's spirit became stronger after death. Physical symptoms of illness, including partial paralysis, were his not unsurprising psychological responses to fear of having been bewitched and perhaps also to guilt about his wife's death. Carpenter offered Santainna a counter-charm, two ordinary aspirins, to combat the witchcraft. Shortly after taking the remedy, his paralysis disappeared. By the next day, he had returned to his normal activities.

After 1950 Aivilik economic and social conditions began to improve. Tuberculosis was controllable through medicines. Government assistance stabilized the economy. The Aivilik were able to improve their housing facilities. And Catholic mission activities provided the Aivilik with new rituals for fear-reduction. As intense stresses of life eased on these several fronts, the fear of witches faded. Today the Aivilik give much less emphasis to mystical causation of events because there is a greater understanding of natural reasons.

The Aivilik are not alone in using witchcraft as an explanation of life's misfortunes. Several anthropologists who have examined the prevalence of witchcraft beliefs in different cultures have determined that similar social stresses underlie such beliefs. Whiting (1950) found that the use of magic to cause harm to others was likely in societies that lacked "individuals or groups of individuals with delegated authority to settle disputes" (p. 90). In other words, witchcraft was common where retaliation by peers was the main tool of social control. Whiting and Child (1953) found that a belief in witches who have innate supernatural abilities to harm others was most common in societies where the socialization of children causes them anxiety about their ability to control aggression or sexuality.

In a statistical comparison of a number of societies from around the world, Swanson (1960) found support for Whiting and Child's ideas. He found that belief in the evil magic was most common in societies where individuals lacked socially approved means for protecting themselves from the actions of those with whom they had to interact. Societies like the Aivilik, in which there was no traditional police force or judicial system to turn to when one person violated another's rights are the ones most likely to believe in witchcraft. Similar beliefs were common in New England during the famous Salem witchcraft trials when the American legal system was particularly weak. And resident witchcraft beliefs became popular again in the 1960s and 1970s during another period of political turmoil. Thus, the Aivilik were not alone in their intensified belief in witchcraft as a way to explain an increasing number of problems. Ironically, as their problems increased in number, the witchcraft belief itself became a major social problem.

■ References

Carpenter, E. S. (1953). Witch-fear among the Aivilik Eskimos. *American Journal of Psychiatry*, *11*(3), 149-199.

Kemper, T. D. (1978). *A social interactional theory of emotions*. New York: Wiley.

Swanson, G. (1960). *The birth of the gods: The origin of primitive belief*. Ann Arbor, MI: University of Michigan Press.

Whiting, B. (1950). *Paiute sorcery* (No. 15). New York: Viking Fund Publications in Anthropology.

Whiting, J. W. M., & , Child, I. L. (1953). *Child training and personality: A cross-cultural study*. New Haven, CT: Yale University Press.

■ Discussion Questions

1. How does the concept of witchcraft differ from medical explanations of "natural" deaths?

2. Why did the fear of witches rather suddenly arise among the Aivilik? What function did it serve?

3. What social conditions seem to make it easier for a group to accept the idea of witchcraft or sorcery?

■ For Further Exploration

1. Review the description of generalized anxiety disorders. What conditions in our culture might predispose an individual to this disorder? What role do belief systems play in eliciting various emotional responses?

■ For Additional Reading

Whiting, B. (1950). *Paiute sorcery* (No. 15). New York: Viking Fund Publications in Anthropology. An ethnographic account of the role of magic in Paiute society.

The Elderly in Native American Culture

■ Stimulus Question

Few groups have had to change more over the past 150 years than Native Americans. What roles do elderly Native Americans have in their families now that their cultures have adjusted to modern life in the United States?

W HEN Lee and Kezis (1968) studied the status of older people around the world, they found that in all cultures, the elderly had low status when certain social traits were present. For instance, when people live in *nuclear families* (just the two parents and their children) it is hard for old people to maintain their role as family heads. By the time they are old, their children have left home and have founded their own, independent families. Older people are likely to have higher status when people live in *extended families* (including more relatives than just the nuclear family). They also tend to keep their higher status in societies where ancestry and inheritance are determined through only one parent. When wealth or position may be acquired from either parent, then the power of older family members is diluted.

According to Cowgill (1972), older people enjoyed a privileged position in preliterate societies around the world. With relatively few people living to a very old age, those who did held a special, venerable position. In many cases, they were the "wise ones" who led the group, and held knowledge about the past to pass on to younger generations. What distinguished them from the elderly in industrialized societies was that they remained functional within the group—useful and needed individuals. With all its wonderful technological advances, industrialization has also caused a general lowering of older people's status and a reduction in the number of roles they play. Today, both the number of aged people and the percentage of the population who are aged have increased, making old age a less unique stage of life. Due to modernization and rapid technological change, the functions once performed by the elderly are no longer needed.

In traditional Native American culture, old age was an important time of life where a number of important tasks had to be performed. Old age security was, in part, a result of possessing property and being a reservoir of skills and special knowledge that were necessary for the well-being of the group. For instance, the elderly were usually responsible for younger people's graduation to adulthood. They were also responsible for the entertainment, education, and moral instruction of their society, provided through stories, songs, games, and dances. The role of religious specialist was also one most likely held by the elderly. The extended family made it easy for grandparents and grandchildren to have had a very special relationship in which the grandparents often served as surrogate parents.

Today elderly Native Americans have a number of disadvantages compared to other groups of aged people. Over half have incomes below the poverty level. Only 14% of those over 65 years of age have a high school education. And the average life expectancy of Native Americans is about seven years less than that of whites (Schweitzer, 1983). A number of sociological factors have also harmed the position of the aged: The extended family is being replaced by the nuclear family; and like other American families, Native American families are becoming residentially mobile. Along with these changes, young Native Americans have begun to adopt many U.S. values in which the family plays a less significant role than it did for their parents.

Marjorie Schweitzer (1983) has examined the position of the elderly in two Oklahoma tribes: the Oto-Missouri and the Ioway. These two tribes are linguistically, culturally, and historically related. Both tend to define old age more by roles than by chronological age. People are "old" if they function politically as elders in the tribe, hold knowledge about tribal ways and customs, or are grandparents within the family or head of the household. The elderly who serve in these roles receive honor and respect because of the functions that they serve. People are also "old" when they can no longer take care of themselves.

The Oto and Ioway elderly experience a relatively positive old age even in contemporary times. Two important roles exist for them, one within the extended family and the other at the public tribal level. Specific roles include those of ritual specialist at naming ceremonies, religious specialists in the Native American Church, and masters of ceremonies at tribal dances. Furthermore, it is their role to share traditional knowledge, teach their language, and pass down songs and legends to the young. Since emphasis on traditional ways has remained important, the elderly have a function only they can fulfill. Consequently, they hold prestige and power within the family. The Oto and Ioway teach their young to value and respect old people. Furthermore, it is customary for grandparents to raise grandchildren if anything happens to their parents. Grandchildren in return provide special services to their grandparents out of love and respect. In the extended family system, there is always someone to fill the role of grandparent even when one's biological grandparents are no longer living. The grandparent role is so important that when a grandparent dies, an older friend of the deceased may take over that role.

Among the Oto and Ioway, being dependent on other family members does not carry negative connotations. It is not uncommon for three generations of to live near one another. Adult children may move back to the reservation when they reach middle age to be closer to aged parents. Even when elders become dependent, they still make their own decisions and keep the respect of others.

Although residential mobility and migration have weakened family structure, even in these two tribes, summer encampments or "powwows" offer an opportunity for extended families to reunite. When a boy becomes eligible to dance publicly, it is his grandfather who places the ceremonial headdress on the boy's head. Grandfather then walks with the boy in a circle around the drums and singers, symbolizing the "going-around-together" of the old and the young. This bond between grandparent and grandchild creates continuity from generation to generation.

Clearly, elderly Native Americans who maintain a position of respect and importance in their society are found in groups that continue to hold on to traditional values—values that assign an important function to the elderly. In groups that have moved away from their heritage, the role of the aged approximates that of the aged in the United States at large.

■ References

Cowgill, D.O. (1972). A theory of aging in cross-cultural perspective. In D. Cowgill & L. Holmes (Eds.), *Aging and modernization* (pp. 1-13). New York: Appleton-Century-Crofts.

Lee, G. R., & Kezis, M. (1968). Family structure and the status of the elderly. *Journal of Comparative Family Studies, 10,* 420-443.

Schweitzer, M.M. (1983). The elders: Cultural dimensions of aging in two American Indian communities. In J. Sokolovsky (Ed.), *Growing old in different societies: Cross-cultural perspectives.* Belmont, CA: Wadsworth.

■ Discussion Questions

1.   What factors distinguish the elderly in nonindustrialized societies from those living in the industrialized West?

2.   How is the role of the elderly in Native American societies changing?

3.   Why is old age for the Oto and the Ioway relatively positive?

4.   What have been the main causes of change in the roles of Native Americans?

■ For Further Exploration

1.   Identify the roles and functions of the typical older adult in your own society. Would it be appropriate to identify late life as a role-less time in your own society?

■ For Additional Reading

Sokolovsky, J. (Ed.). (1983). *Growing old in different societies: Cross-cultural perspectives.* Belmont, CA: Wadsworth. A collection of articles on aging in various societies.

Female Initiation Rites

■ Stimulus Question

Although they are unusual in American culture, initiation ceremonies for adolescents have existed in most of the world's societies throughout history. What purposes do such rites serve?

ADOLESCENCE—the bridge between childhood and adulthood—is a time of many physical and psychological changes. It is a time of searching for an identity as an independent adult, a quest that is probably more important than any other in life. Erikson (1963) has described the central task of adolescence as replacing role confusion with a secure sense of personal identity. Adolescents must redefine themselves in ways that will help them negotiate their future life course. An adolescent is in the process of acquiring an occupational identity, an ideological identity, and a sexual identity—producing what has been described by some as an "identity crisis."

Everett Dulit (1988, p. 16) has described the psychological tasks that Americans are faced with during adolescence. Increased sexual feelings must be mastered. Aggressive impulses must be controlled. Dependency on parents and peers must be gradually replaced with personal independence. In the process, the adolescent tries to retain the sense of being special that was previously associated with childhood roles. This is a time for developing new skills that will be needed in the future, and for preparing to shift the most important feelings of love from family to chosen partners. While negotiating all these changes, the adolescent must come to terms with a complicated series of bodily changes as well.

These are the key issues of adolescence in American society. Most stage theorists suggest that it is the successful mastery of these tasks that sets up the adolescent entry into the adult world. Are these, however, the tasks of adolescents everywhere? Are the changes of adolescence so universally fraught with difficulties that it is correct to think of this as a period inevitably characterized by turmoil and identity crises? Some contend that the turmoil of adolescence in American society is not a natural consequence of developmental processes, but rather stems from our lack of customs to ease the transition from childhood to adult roles.

Most of the societies that have been studied by cultural anthropologists have important public ceremonies to mark the transition from child to adult. This is in stark contrast to the American approach, which leaves children to their own devices in finding their identities. Without a clearly defined procedure to follow, this process can be difficult: Parents may interpret independent behavior as a rejection of the values they have taught and may struggle to keep a child in a dependent role. Peers may demand that the adolescent prove his or her independence by certain dangerous behaviors. So adolescence is a time of testing skills at negotiating one's wants and needs with friends and family.

Consider for a moment how much easier this transition would be if American society weren't so vague about what it means to "grow up." In America adult rights are doled out piecemeal. Driving rights are granted at age sixteen, voting and marrying rights are granted at age eighteen, and the right to buy alcohol at twenty-one. American society gives no clear message about when a child really becomes an adult. However, in many of the world's societies the complete transition to adulthood is officially approved and celebrated at a particular age, often through a particular ceremony or procedure. And many anthropologists believe that there is much less turmoil, rebellion, and confusion for adolescents this way.

Cohen (1964) looked at 65 nonindustrialized societies from around the world and found that 45 of them held adulthood ceremonies. They were the least elaborate among those that had the simplest kinds of family group, such as the so-called nuclear family that Americans are familiar with, consisting of only the two parents and their children. The societies that had large extended families of grandparents, children, and grandchildren who lived and worked together had the most elaborate ceremonies to mark a child's move into new adult roles. These adulthood celebrations were seen to benefit society at large by promoting respect for its customs rather than casting the adolescent into a rebellious role.

In societies where adult skills were hard or dangerous, or where father-son ties were weak but men had to cooperate in hard work as adults, the manhood rituals were dramatic and painful. The male puberty rituals allowed the boy to prove to the community—and to himself— that he had what it takes to be a man.

Brown (1963) found similar things when she looked at those societies that practiced "rites of passage" for girls, ceremonies in which they were proclaimed to have become young women. Brown defined female initiation rites as those that "consist of one or more prescribed ceremonial events, mandatory for all girls of a given society, and celebrated between their eighth and twentieth years" (p. 838). She chose 75 societies for which sufficient information was available concerning the adolescent life of girls. Geographically, this sample of societies represented groups from all major regions of the world: 14 were African societies, 10 were from the Insular Pacific, 13 were pre-European North American societies, and 16 societies were from South America. Forty-three of these groups practiced female initiation rites that met the criteria of Brown's definition.

Three reasons appear to be most important to understanding why special rites for young women take place in some societies and not in others. Initiation rites are most common in societies where the young girl continues to reside and work in her mother's home after marriage. The ritual emphasizes the importance of change in girls' behavior as they become women, and of change in the ways that other people in the group will henceforth treat them. The puberty ceremony helps the girl overcome her established habits of childhood and aids the transition to her new role—which must take place in the same environment as her old role. Among the Bimba of Zimbabwe, for example, "the girl is told that she has to do things with a new spirit and a new sense of responsibility . . . these rites are the means by which the girl publicly accepts her new legal role" (p. 841).

In societies where young women move away from their family's location when they marry, female initiation rites are unlikely to occur. This is true when women leave home to set up a new residence near their husbands' families so the husbands can continue to contribute to the work of their families. It is also the case when the couple finds an entirely new location to work and live. Thus, American society's lack of puberty rituals conforms to the general pattern, since children usually leave home and find places of their own to live and work. However, female adulthood rituals are common even in societies where a woman only returns to her parents' home intermittently—for instance, to help at harvest time. And such rites do exist among some societies in which a young woman permanently leaves home. In these societies, the rituals tend to be painful and may involve genital operations or extensive tattooing, especially if girls customarily slept with their mother as children. Brown believes that this close identification of a girl with her mother creates a sexual identity problem when she establishes her role as an independently functioning adult. The identity problem is particularly acute if a woman's new life requires a shift of residence to the household of her husband where life revolves around men who cooperate in heavy labor. In such situations, her life will have changed from one of comfortable identification and dependence on her mother to one of isolation and subordination to nonrelatives. Painful female initiation rites dramatically help the girl understand that she must make the transition from dependent child to a woman who will have to fend for herself in a male-dominated environment.

Rites of passage appear to be linked to three aspects of life in nonindustrialized societies: (a) where young adults will live after they marry, (b) how important their adult work will be to the group where they were reared, and (c) the likelihood of confusion or conflict in young people about their sexual identities or the shift from nurtured dependence to fending for themselves. The purpose of such rites is to help the adolescent—and those around him or her—acknowledge a change to new responsibilities and rights, which occur for all young people regardless of culture. Societies that do practice initiation rites employ them as part of a process to enable both the individual and society to adjust to change and enjoy a sense of continuity.

■ References

Brown, J. K. (1963). A cross-cultural study of female initiation rites. *American Anthropologist, 65,* 837-853.

Cohen, Y. A. (1964). *The transition from childhood to adolescence: Cross-cultural studies in initiation ceremonies, legal systems, and incest taboos.* Chicago: Aldine.

Dulit, E. (1988). In R. Brescia (Ed.), Psychiatry of adolescence. *Videotaped review of American psychiatry.* Pelham, NY: Specialty Preparation.

Erikson, E. H. (1963). *Childhood and society* (2nd ed.). New York: Norton.

■ Discussion Questions

1. What purposes do female initiation rites serve in primitive societies?

2. Why might role confusion exist for adolescent females in some nonindustrialized societies?

3. Do you think many differences exist between the psychological tasks of adolescents in Western societies and young people in less socially complex societies? Would Brescia's list of psychological tasks be equally appropriate for adolescents in Third World countries?

■ For Further Exploration

1. Collect information on American groups that do practice an adulthood ritual such as a "Sweet Sixteen" or "Coming Out" party or a *Bar Mitzvah* or *Bat Mitzvah*. Discuss whether these groups really are exceptions to what anthropologists have found elsewhere or whether they actually fit the general pattern.

■ For Additional Reading

Van Gennep, A. (1960). *The rites of passage.* (S. T. Kimball, Trans.). Chicago: University of Chicago Press. The classic discussion of all the major life changes that people celebrate at various times in a person's life cycle.

Race, Culture, and IQ

■ Stimulus Questions

Just how much does environment affect a child's IQ? Are differences between racial groups in IQ test achievement due to inborn differences in intellectual skills or environmental conditions in upbringing?

E XPLAINING racial differences in IQ scores has always been a thorny problem. Typically, minority groups tend to perform less well than nonminority members of society on such tests and this is true whether the minority groups are racially different or not. In the United States, for instance, an ethnic group such as Eastern European immigrants who are racially Caucasian might perform below the average of the dominant members of the same race. In such a case we would have to explain the test-result differences by pointing to the environmental differences between the two groups. Since racial minorities have lower incomes than white Americans overall, they also suffer environmental differences. Racial minorities are more likely to live in the poor part of town where the schools have smaller budgets and a harder time recruiting the best teachers. In addition, the cultural background of racial minorities is often different from that which is taught (and tested) in the schools (Crapo, 1987, pp. 83-90). Often the language or the dialect spoken in the child's home is different as well. Environment, therefore, appears to account for racial differences in IQ test performance. But racial minorities are also culturally and socially different from the dominant nonminority white race. So some psychologists have occasionally asked whether race might also contribute to the lower IQ test performance.

Studying racial differences in IQ test performance poses a serious problem due to the pervasiveness of racial prejudice. It is important for researchers to be aware of the effect of racial prejudice when looking for evidence of true racial differences, such as genetic differences between the races' natural abilities. Research can be methodologically flawed. And sometimes researchers simply "discover" what their prejudices lead them to expect.

Let's start with a case in point. For many years, IQ test data has indicated that African-American children score on the average, 15 points lower than white children. Several well-established perspectives have been taken on why this particular phenomenon exists. The "nature vs. nurture" positions have never had a richer topic for the discussion of their respective points of view. One group takes the stance that intellectual capacity is primarily genetically determined (Jensen, 1981). Others strongly advocate an environmental explanation for IQ differences since it is well known that an impoverished environment can reduce a person's intellectual attainment.

One way to sort out this "nature vs. nurture" controversy is to compare racially different children who have very similar social environments. For instance, we should make comparisons between African-American and white children whose families have the same kinds of educational background, occupations, and the same levels of income. We should not compare children from intact families with children from divorced or one-parent families. We should also minimize other "environmental" differences. If the test performance of the two groups then continues to show the same differences, the idea that the differences were caused by genetics becomes more plausible. Another way to assess the effects of environment and genetics would be to compare children who have different social environments. If there were little difference between the IQ scores of the two groups, we would conclude that heredity had played a strong role in test performance. On the other hand, if the racially identical children in the two different social groups performed very differently, then the differences would be attributable to environment.

Zena Blau (1981) compared 579 black and 523 white mothers and their fifth- and sixth-grade children in communities around Chicago. Overall, the two groups differed by 10 IQ points. But when Blau compared black children with white children of similar social and economic rank, the scores of the white children averaged only 6 points higher than those of the black children. So when only two environmental factors were minimized, the gap declined by 40%! The clear implication is that if other social differences were taken into account, the gap would become still smaller or would disappear entirely.

Hofstadter (1963) showed that religious background also influences the intellectual development of children. For instance, evangelical fundamentalist churches foster anti-intellectualism through their opposition to science, modern secular education, and the kind of life that industrialization and urbanization have caused. As you would expect, the anti-intellectual values of these churches affect the intellectual performance of children who grow up in them. African-American children are much more likely to grow up in fundamentalist religious environments than are white children in the United States. So the religious influence on IQ performance may be an important one, maybe even as important as the black-white differences caused by economic and social standing.

In Blau's study, two-thirds of the black students were from a fundamentalist background. So what would happen to the six-point difference that remained between her economically and socially similar black and white students if only those of similar religious background were compared? Blau tried to answer this question by comparing black and white students of similar socioeconomic *and* religious backgrounds. When this was done, the difference between the average IQ scores of the two groups was only four points. There were no differences at all between the average scores of high socioeconomic-status Protestants, nondenominational students, and nonreligious students. In other words, race was irrelevant to IQ performance for these social groups.

Scarr (1981) took the approach of comparing children from the same race who were raised in very different environments. She found even more dramatic evidence for the effects of environment than did Blau or Hofstadter. Scarr suggested that if black children who were raised in a white world do better on IQ tests than blacks raised in black environments, then environment would be a sufficient explanation of so-called "racial differences" in IQ scores. African-American children adopted by white families offer a way of answering this question.

Scarr and Weinberg (1975, 1976) studied 101 white families who had adopted black children in the Minneapolis area. She collected data about home environment and IQs of all family members. Within this sample there were 130 black children who had been adopted and 145 black children who lived with their birth families. Scarr gave the Stanford-Binet test to children who were from four to eight years of age and the Wechsler Intelligence Scale for Children (WISC) to those between nine and sixteen. Parents of all the children took the Wechsler Adult Intelligence Scale (WAIS).

Adopted black children's scores averaged 106, but those children who were adopted at an earlier age scored about 110. This number is a full 10 points higher than the average IQ score of the nonadopted black children. The longer the adopted children lived in the environment of their adoptive nonminority, white families, the better the children performed. And the environmental difference brought their performance to a level above the national average. The race of these children had not changed. So Scarr feels justified in attributing the lower-than-average performance of the nonadoptive children to environment rather than any racial difference in capacity. After all, the adopted children's high scores proved that they had the capacity to perform better than the national average.

Did the tremendous increase in IQ scores have a payoff in how these black children performed in school? Apparently so! Scarr's sample of adopted black children scored above average—in the 55th percentile—on national achievement tests in reading and math. In contrast, the general population of black children in the same Minneapolis area scored in the 15th percentile. This comparison attests to a major environmental impact on different members of the same racial group.

Scarr also found that the quality of children's life before adoption also influenced their performance after adoption. The fewer disturbances children have in their lives before they are adopted and the better their care in the first years of life, the higher their later IQs were. Scarr pointed out that children who have parents who are relatively poorly educated and even below average in intelligence can do extremely well if they grow up in an enriched environment.

Scarr tried to characterize the qualities of the adoptive families that might define the nature of the "enriched" environment they provided. Certainly, specific family characteristics also play a role in the development of intelligence for both natural and adopted children. These adoptive families were generally emotionally warm, physically and psychologically comfortable, and free of anxiety. The parents were relaxed with children. Households tended to be run in a democratic fashion with intellectual stimulation available to the children. Scarr believes that all these factors contributed to the child's intellectual attainment.

The black-white IQ gap appears adequately explained by this and other research. It is clear that at least part of everyone's ultimate achievement can be linked to factors in his or her environment, so the important issue now is what are we prepared to do to increase any person's potential.

■ References

Blau, Z. S. (1981). *Black children/white children: Competence, socialization, and social structure.* New York: The Free Press.

Crapo, R. (1987). *Cultural anthropology: Understanding ourselves and others.* Guilford, CT: Dushkin.

Hofstadter, R. (1963). *Anti-intellectualism in American life.* New York: McGraw-Hill.

Jensen, A. R. (1981). *Straight talk about mental tests.* New York: Macmillan.

Scarr, S. (1981). *Race, social class, and individual differences in I.Q.* Hillsdale, NJ: Lawrence Erlbaum.

Scarr-Salapatek, S., & Weinberg, R. A. (1975, December). When black children grow up in white homes. *Psychology Today*, 80-82.

Scarr, S., & Weinberg, R. A. (1976). IQ test performance of black children adopted by white families. *American Psychologist, 31*, 726-739.

■ Discussion Questions

1. How much of a difference did it make in IQ scores when adopted black children were raised in white homes? What other variables also seem to affect intellectual achievement in adoptive situations?

2. From Scarr's research, why would it be difficult to support the idea that black children are genetically disadvantaged in relation to intellectual achievement?

■ For Further Exploration

1. A great deal has been written about the implications of black-white IQ score differences. On the other hand, relatively little has been done to explain why Asian-American children have outperformed white children on various standardized tests given in some American schools. For instance, no one seems to have been motivated to study whether this white "deficit" is best explained by a genetic disadvantage in the white race. And there is no raging argument about whether the discrepancy might be explainable in terms of a cultural impoverishment in child rearing in white homes. What

does this difference in the treatment of the two cases suggest about the role of racism in stimulating controversies over race and intelligence?

■ For Additional Reading

Locurto, C. (1991). *Sense and nonsense about IQ: The case for uniqueness*. New York: Praeger. Covers the history of the IQ controversy from 1884 through 1990.

Scarr, S. (1981). *Race, social class, and individual differences in I.Q.* Hillsdale, NJ: Lawrence Erlbaum. A comprehensive study of what was known about the relationships between genetics, ethnic and racial differences, social class, and intelligence as of 1981.

Leadership Characteristics: The Case of Moral Reasoning in a Rural African Community

■ Stimulus Questions

What if we chose politicians, judges, and other officials for their moral reasoning abilities? What if only the most morally outstanding members of the community were acceptable for public office? Would we still have the same individuals in office or power? Do leaders differ significantly from non-leaders in their moral perspectives?

FOR over twenty years, Kohlberg's theory of moral development and judgment has been a primary tool in explaining how children and adults justify their actions. There is no doubt that people reason at different levels of complexity or that they differ in their skill at considering the welfare of the community over self-interest. As general cognitive capacity develops, moral-reasoning ability does too, progressing through six stages.

It is Kohlberg's claim that stages are culturally universal that is most interesting to cross-cultural researchers. Within any society there are customary values about what behavior is justified or right. But are the forms of moral reasoning that Kohlberg called the "highest" recognized as the best forms in all societies? Over a dozen studies, including one by Kohlberg, suggest that the last two stages are not found in peasant or tribal societies. Therefore, some have suggested that Kohlberg's upper stages of moral judgment only develop where government officials must resolve conflicts and make decisions about people they do not personally know. In less complex societies, "conventional" strategies are quite sufficient to deal with the demands of everyday life.

Harkness, Edwards, and Super (1981) conducted a study of moral judgments in a rural Kipsigis community in western Kenya to explore the relationship between moral reasoning and people's social roles. They wondered whether the men who had a reputation as the "moral leaders" of their people would also be those with the highest level of moral reasoning in Kohlberg's scheme.

The Kipsigis people were simple agriculturalists who lived in a rural area and had little formal education. Although they participated in the national economy by producing cash crops, they maintained a very traditional life. People generally settled disputes at the community level. The major goal of conflict resolution was the restoration of peace in the village. Certain senior men, referred to as *boisiek*, were chosen to resolve conflicts. The boisiek were those who had a reputation for having the verbal skills, the powers of intellectual reasoning, and the recognized moral integrity to best do the job.

Twelve men were interviewed. Six were boisiek. The other six were simply ordinary members of the community, not involved in any major way with village disputes. Although they did not have the same reputation of high moral quality as the boisiek, neither were their reputations negative.

To measure the differences in the reputations of members of these two groups, the researchers asked the twelve participants to name the "most respected men" of the community. Members of the group of leaders were named an average of 5.1 times, while members of the non-leader group were mentioned an average of only 0.5 times.

Harkness and her fellow researchers presented all twelve Kipsigi men with Kohlbergian stories that were modified to fit Kipsigi life. Among other dilemmas, the respondents were asked to decide (a) whether a boy should obey his father and give him some money he had earned himself even though his father had promised the boy that he would be able keep it; (b) who did worse, a boy who stole money from a store or one who conned a trusting old man out of an equal amount; and (c) how to resolve a dilemma similar to the now quite familiar one of Heinz: "Is a man right or wrong to steal a drug to save his dying wife when he can not obtain the drug legally?" The researchers asked each man to respond as if this were the problem before him at a community dispute-settlement meeting.

Leaders and non-leaders tended to agree about how they would resolve the various dilemmas. However, leaders reasoned at a higher moral level on Kohlberg's scale, and with one exception, all leaders scored better than the non-leaders. The number of times others had named them as a respected and honest community leader was the best predictor of respondents' scores on Kohlberg's Moral Maturity scale. This supports the idea that Kohlberg's scale does measure qualities that are recognized by others as evidence of moral leadership. Interestingly, the age, education, wealth, and religious backgrounds of the men had no bearing on how well they scored.

The Kipsigi moral leaders emphasized community well-being over personal gain, an orientation that gave them a higher score on the scale. The moral leaders also scored higher because they were more likely to believe that a man should command respect by being a role model of superior moral qualities, whereas most of the non-leaders emphasized the right of a father or elder to command respect because he had more power than others. Leaders held that people should practice mutual help because it is good for the welfare of the society, not according to some accounting system of give and take. For example, family members should help each other without considering what they hoped to receive in return.

The Kipsigis moral leaders expressed more decisions in ways that put them at the Stage 3 or 4 levels of moral reasoning than did the other men, who made more Stage 1 and 2 judgments, placing greater emphasis on what one might "want" rather than what one "should do." This certainly supports the claim that Kohlberg's scale measures moral differences that people from different societies perceive in the same way. As in similar studies, responses that belonged to Kohlberg's Stages 5 and 6 were absent in the Kipsigis people's solutions to the dilemmas. Did this mean that the Kipsigis were less morally developed than people in the West? Or was Kohlberg wrong in claiming that all six of his stages are part of a universal developmental sequence in humans?

Harkness and her associates argue that only the first four stages are valid as universally recognized levels of moral development. They have suggested that conventional modes of reasoning (Stages 3 and 4) are appropriate for the demands of this Kenyan society. The Kipsigis community is small and has relatively stable relationships over time. Theirs was not the experience of an urban faceless crowd in which the moral order of society was maintained by a government whose officials had no personal relationship with those they governed. So, the Kipsigis' social system has no need for the kind of reasoning that is used in industrialized societies. In other words, Kohlberg's highest scores reflect the values of an industrialized lifestyle, not an inherently superior form of morality.

■ References

Harkness, S., Edwards, C.P., & Super, C.M. (1981). Social roles and moral reasoning: A case study in a rural African community. *Developmental Psychology*, *17*, 595-603.

■ Discussion Questions

1. What traits differentiated leaders from non-leaders in the Kipsigis village?

2. What relationship existed between an individual's level of moral reasoning and his social role in the Kipsigis society?

3. Does the absence of Stage 5 and 6 levels of moral reasoning among the Kipsigis contradict Kohlberg's belief that these stages are culturally universal?

4. Can you point to any individuals you know whose social roles reflect their moral character?

■ For Further Exploration

1. Review Kohlberg's descriptions of how people would respond to the following dilemma according to their level of moral reasoning. "Should a boy obey his father and give him the money he had earned himself even though his father had previously promised he could keep it?" How would someone at each of Kohlberg's levels of moral reasoning decide this problem?

■ For Additional Reading

Nader, L., & Todd, H. F. (1978). *The disputing process: Law in ten societies*. New York: Columbia University Press. Laura Nader and Henry Todd provide comparative information about how legal decisions are made in rural Third World communities and in the industrialized West.

Age Differences in Personality Traits Among the Highland Maya

■ Stimulus Questions

Our personalities change throughout our lives. Is there a universal sequence to these changes? For instance, are the changes that happen to American men throughout their lives similar to male life changes in other cultures?

D AVID GUTMANN (1967) carried out a study that suggests there is a universal sequence to the changes that people go through as they age. He identified three stages that American men go through. In each stage, the individual sees himself and those around him in certain ways, has specific drives, and uses certain defenses. Typically, from the age of 40 to about 54 he concerns himself with control of his world. During this period, he strives for independence and achievement, particularly in his work and in associated interpersonal interactions. From ages 55 to 70 he attempts to accommodate his world. He now recognizes that it is necessary to change himself rather than the world around him. His achievement drive and the need for autonomy decline. Finally, after 70, he begins to use more regressive defensive strategies such as denial and projection to maintain his self-esteem and security. He no longer sees the world as a place where he exercises control.

Gutmann chose forty Highland Maya men in the Mexican state of Chiapas to compare with Americans by means of interviews supplemented with projective tests. These nonliterate, subsistence-level corn farmers, who ranged in age from 30 to 90, resided in remote villages. Gutmann searched particularly for the psychological dimensions of contentment and discontentment, relief, vitality, and death. He was especially interested in the respondents' views of the future and their views of old men's roles. He also tried to learn how contentment was gained, lost, and then regained. He studied the dreams of these Maya men and how they lost or conserved their vitality in late life.

Gutmann found definite age-related differences in how the Maya men reacted to the question, "What makes you happy?" Men over 50 were more passive-dependent and explicitly oral than men under 50, who often gave answers related to productive work. The older group deemphasized productivity and achievement and instead mentioned avoiding physical threats, not getting ill, and staying out of trouble. Happiness, for the older respondents, came from viewing something beautiful, visiting friends and family, drinking, listening to music, and having sufficient food. When Gutmann asked them what made them unhappy, the younger respondents referred to losses or interruptions in their work due to illness, injury, or unfortunate circumstances. The competitive struggle to be successful, or at least to have what one needs, was a recurrent theme. In contrast, older men were most often unhappy if they were physically or emotionally deprived, or if there was a loss of food supplies. Whereas younger men were most worried about the "market" conditions, older men focused on their family, friends, food, and physical maintenance.

Next, Gutmann asked, "When you are unhappy, how do you make yourself happy again?" Three general ways of restoring lost contentment were mentioned: (a) through one's own efforts, (b) through reliance on an omnipotent figure, and (c) through oral means of gaining satisfaction. Again, Gutmann found age differences. Younger men relied much more heavily on their own instrumental actions to alleviate discontentment. Work was often the remedy for such a problem. Although a large percentage of older men also stressed their own involvement in solving problems (with comments such as, "I cure myself and so am happy again"), many believed in omnipotent-types of external figures to turn things around: the Virgin Mary, doctors, and even soldiers (to restore order and peace in the area). By a wide margin, older Maya also believed in the restorative powers of food, drink, and medicine (their oral orientation). This data indicated the most significant shift was from self-reliance to a dependence on external sources of satisfaction, such as powerful people or food and drink. The men's psychological "locus of control" shifted from internal to external as they aged.

Fifteen of the respondents reported dreams. Gutmann categorized these dreams as either representing "mastery" which included work and the acceptance of loss, or "passivity" involving helplessness, dying, and external attacks. There were significant differences between age groups. Seventy-one percent of the dreams of older men dealt with themes of passivity. In contrast, younger men tended to have dreams in which their ego was securely in control of what happened in their dreams. Gutmann suggests that the older men's dreams may indicate the unconscious wish to be dominated by powerful external forces.

Finally, Gutmann allowed the Maya men to ask the researchers questions to see what differences might arise regarding the types of questions raised by each age group. Younger men asked "objective" questions related to the interviewer's work, pay, and training. Older men asked more self-referent questions wanting to know why the interviewer asked questions and who would hear the tapes. Older men were also more skeptical of the interviewers—to the point of viewing them as morally deviant since they didn't work hard in the corn fields! Gutmann suggests that this shift in later life to a more referential thinking style may be tied to a changed concept of death. At a significant level, older men believed in supernatural explanations, including witchcraft, to explain death. Personal-referent causes such as envy, witchcraft, and retribution for sins were given as explanations for someone's death. They interpreted events in terms of their personal relevance. Thus, death was not due to some impersonal cause, but rather the result of personal malice, perhaps involving a supernatural agent.

The major conclusion that can be reached from this study of Highland Maya men is that age differences in ego states are similar despite different cultures. The Maya and Americans both progressed through the same stages of mastery as they grew older. Older subjects had a more passive-dependent orientation, a more external locus of control, and a stronger oral interest than did younger men. Furthermore, in a related study, Gutmann found similar changes associated with age from the lowland Maya of the Yucatan. From three samples of aging men, certain personality shifts appear to take place despite very different cultural surroundings.

■ References

Gutmann, D. (1967). Aging among the Highland Maya: A comparative study. *Journal of Personality and Social Psychology, 7*, 28-35.

■ Discussion Questions

1. According to Gutmann, what personality shifts can American men expect to experience as they age?
2. What differences were noted between older and younger Maya men in Gutmann's study?
3. How can you link dreams and personality together to better understand the individual?
4. What was Gutmann's conclusion concerning universal personality shifts with age?

■ For Further Exploration

1. Gutmann's study was an example of cross-sectional research that compared several age groups at one time. What errors of interpretation could this approach lead to that a longitudinal approach to psychological change would avoid?

■ For Additional Reading

Gutmann, D. (1966). Mayan aging—A comparative TAT study. *Psychiatry, 29*, 246-259.

Witchcraft!

■ Stimulus Question

On a societal level, what conditions could cause enough anxiety, frustration, and mental stress that people would look toward witchcraft to alleviate them?

IT would be fair to say that specific groups of people develop rather idiosyncratic ways of managing stress. Stress itself comes from many sources that may be common across cultures, but adaptation to the stressors may be culture specific. Consider the "fitness craze" that has spread throughout the United States. In part, it is a way many Americans cope with stress.

S. F. Nadel (1952) has examined the practice of witchcraft as a stress reliever among African groups. The Nupe and the Gwari of Northern Nigeria and the Korongo and the Mesakin of Central Sudan were studied. These people are similar in many ways, but they have very different approaches to witchcraft, and one tribe, the Korongo, does not practice it.

Within the Nupe tribe, strong sex-antagonism exists. This antagonism goes back even into "ancient times" as exemplified by legends depicting a certain inequality between the sexes—with women in a position superior to that of men. Among the Nupe, it is primarily women who practice witchcraft, although men can, too. The Nupe consider witchcraft to be evil, a process in which the witch eats the victim's "life-soul." Witches practice their evil at night, when they send their "shadow-souls" to attack the victim. A few Nupe men possess the *eshe*, a power that is used to combat witchcraft. To achieve greatest power, a witch must work in conjunction with a man possessing eshe who crosses over to become her assistant. This then makes her power deadly. A secret male society has the role of cleansing the village of witchcraft in an annual ritual.

Nupe men have the power to reduce witchcraft but they are also the primary target of it. Generally an older witch will attack a younger man. Nadel believes that hostility between the sexes is at the root of Nupe ideas about witchcraft and the anti-witchcraft activities of the secret male society. Part of the stress experienced by Nupe men is due to women holding a stronger economic position in their society. Many Nupe women are successful itinerant traders and so hold an independent and domineering position in Nupe society that leads men to feel help-less. Women have assumed the role of head of the household and conse-quently pay for many expenses that men traditionally would have. The resentment caused by this role reversal leads Nupe men to blame the women and their witchcraft for anything bad that befalls them.

Among the neighboring Gwari such sex antagonism does not exist. Witchcraft is very much present, but both men and women are victims, and both sexes work to discover the source of the witchcraft. The whole community partakes in the annual cleansing ritual. Marriage in Gwari society is relatively tension-free. Unlike the Nupe, witchcraft does not appear to be a response to stress and hostility between husbands and wives.

In the Central Sudan two neighboring groups with very similar social structures also demonstrate marked differences in their witchcraft —that is, one group believes in witchcraft and the other does not. The belief in witchcraft arises from the dynamics of the life-cycle and the acceptance of the aging process. Both of these groups practice a system of "age-classes" in which a person's membership in a certain age-class defines his or her rights and responsibilities in life. The Mesakin, who believe in witchcraft, have only three age classes: children, unmarried youths, and men (or women). In contrast, the Korongo, who do not believe in witchcraft, have an age-class system of six divisions. It distin-guishes between younger married men who do not yet have children, family-heads with children, and old men.

The Korongo do not believe in witchcraft. This may be due in part to their attitudes toward the fate of growing old. Their system of six age classes allows people to pass through the stages of life with fewer abrupt status changes.

Activities among the Korongo men, especially physical ones indicating strength and virility, do not just suddenly cease. The transition to adulthood and to the status of old age is gradual. It is not uncommon to see older Korongo men still engaged in wrestling and spear-throwing activities along with the younger men in the tribe. The situation is quite opposite for the Mesakin who obsessively fear witchcraft (*torogo*) and have frequent violent confrontations due to it. Only maternal kin practice witchcraft against one another. Quarrels often arise between a mother's brother and sister's son.

Both tribes practice "anticipated inheritance" but whereas a Korongo man passes on a gift of cattle to a sister's son gladly, the Mesakin find the practice an occasion for conflict and fighting. If a younger man takes ill, dies, or suffers some tragedy, witchcraft (torogo) practiced by his uncle is suspected. Among the Mesakin there must always be a reason for witchcraft and the process of anticipatory inheritance is sufficient to invoke it. Part of this antagonism is due to older men resenting growing old and their envy for youth's vitality and virility. In a system of only three age-classes, a Mesakin man goes from the activities of wrestling, spear-fighting, and living in the cattle camps to a more sedate position of family head. For the Mesakin old age may start even while one is still in his 20's and not yet ready to give up activities just begun and valued. This early social advancement into "old age" has created an observed antagonism between young and old, with witchcraft used as an explanation for some of the problems that arise from that antagonism.

In two cases we see witchcraft as a mechanism for venting frustrations toward another group of people within the tribe. For the Nupe the greatest tension exists between men and women due to the status of the women in their tribe. The role of the men's secret society is that of cleansing the village of witchcraft practiced by women against men (perhaps a societal example of Freudian projection). The Mesakin, who are extremely sensitive to the threat of witchcraft, believe that its practice stems from antagonisms between young and old. However, at the base of this antagonism is a societal perspective and system where a man enters the last stage of life well before he is ready.

In both cases, witchcraft has become a response in answer to the tensions between internal groups—male/female, young/old. Whether witchcraft is really responsible for the troubles that befall an individual could certainly be questioned. However, witchcraft does give people a mechanism for channeling anger and frustrations toward others.

Whiting (1950) studied the role of sorcery accusations among the Paiute Indians of North America and concluded that sorcery beliefs and practices filled the void created by a lack of any effective secular means to enforce people's legal rights. This relationship between a weak system of legal controls and the belief in supernatural powers by which humans may achieve their ends has been supported by Swanson (1960), who made a statistical comparison of a cross-cultural sample of societies.

The studies by Nadel and Swanson both imply that societal tensions lead people to project their anxieties about various forms of powerlessness into beliefs about sinister supernatural powers that can be controlled to achieve human ends. The witch, a person with the innate power to harm others, is an apt symbol for the aggression of pent up sexual tensions, which the sorcerer, whose harmful magical powers can be channeled against aggressive people to enforce conformity to societal rules, functions much like a judge or police officer in secular life.

■ References

Nadel, S.F. (1952). Witchcraft in four African societies: An essay in comparison. *American Anthropologist, 54*, 18-29.

Swanson, G. (1960). *The birth of the gods: The origin of primitive belief.* Ann Arbor, MI: University of Michigan Press.

Whiting, B. (1950). *Paiute sorcery (No. 15).* New York: Viking Fund Publications in Anthropology.

■ Discussion Questions

1.   How does Nadel explain the Nupe practice of witchcraft?

2.   How do the Korongo and Mesakin differ in the way "age-classes" and the general process of aging affect interpersonal relationships?

3.   Overall, what societal conditions can be singled out as responsible for contributions to the mental stress felt by these African people?

■ For Further Exploration

1.   Discuss beliefs that you hold that create tension, frustration, and stress with others. Are these beliefs specific to American culture or could they be considered universal?

■ For Additional Reading

Kluckhohn, C. (1940). *Navaho witchcraft (Papers of the Peabody Museum of American Archeology and Ethnology, Harvard University* Vol. 22, No. 2). Cambridge, MA: Harvard University Press. Discusses the ways that Navajos categorized the different forms of witchcraft that their culture recognized.

Whiting, B. (1950). *Paiute sorcery (No. 15).* New York: Viking Fund Publications in Anthropology. A detailed description of the role of sorcery in a Great Basin Native American society.

Coping Styles Among German and Israeli Adolescents

■ Stimulus Questions

Do young people from different cultures vary in how they cope with day-to-day problem situations? How much of a role does environment or cultural history play in the choice of coping strategies?

ADOLESCENCE is a difficult time of life in which a person must build a new identity and learn to deal with family and friends in different ways than before. In addition to becoming more independent and self-reliant, the adolescent must acquire new skills and formulate opinions on ideological subjects (such as religion and politics). The stresses produced by these challenges are coped with in three basic ways all over the world: The adolescents may reach out for advice from others, turn inward to find solutions within themselves, or simply withdraw from unpleasant situations.

The customs of a society can encourage individuals to adopt one of these coping strategies more than another. One society may devote a lot of effort to promoting an active "reaching out for help" approach, emphasizing the importance of tradition, following the wisdom of elders, and turning to specialists who can provide answers. Another society may emphasize people's needs for self-reliance and autonomous decision-making. People in this culture may prefer a more "internal" and contemplative approach to solving problems. Still a third society may send repeated messages about the benefits of avoiding confrontations and getting away from problems.

Seiffge-Krenke and Shulman (1990) did a study of cultural differences in coping by comparing German and Israeli adolescents. All were between 15 and 17 years of age and were similar to one another in many other ways. They were asked to describe how they would cope with the following situations: (a) bad grades, (b) conflicts with parents, (c) conflicts with teachers (d) fear of rejection by peers, (e) difficulties with the opposite sex, (f) dissatisfaction with themselves, (g) anxiety about occupational training, and (h) trouble about use of leisure time. For each kind of problem, they were asked whether they agreed or disagreed with various coping strategies such as: "I discuss the problem with my parents," "I try to get help from institutions," "I behave as if everything is alright," "I try to forget my problems with alcohol or drugs," or "I think about problems and try to find different solutions." The researchers classified the students' responses to these questions as (a) passive (withdrawal), (b) active (using social resources), or (c) internal (using personal cognitive skills).

The German and Israeli styles of coping with problems were definitely different. German youth preferred the active approach of seeking advice from other sources first. They took action to confront their problems through discussions with others and by seeking various forms of social support. They sought answers from institutional sources. They read magazines for ideas about how to cope. In other words, German youths sought various forms of social support to solve their problems. They felt that seeking help from social institutions was a very acceptable option when they needed assistance. To German adolescents, the knowledge they needed was "out there" and could be found either from people or institutions. The second preference of German adolescents—particularly older ones—was to think out a solution themselves, drawing on their own inner resources to find a solution. Apparently their reliance on reflection and personal cognitive skill increased with age. Withdrawal from problem situations was the least popular choice of coping strategy.

Israeli adolescents chose withdrawal even less than the Germans. Their preferred method of coping was the internal approach of thinking through a solution on their own. These young people relied more on their cognitive processes to reduce stress than on outside help. In fact, they used an internal coping approach nearly twice as much as the Germans. Also, unlike the Germans, when they did seek help it was from friends, peers, and informal social networks, not impersonal social institutions.

There were also interesting differences in the approach to particular situations. Although both groups used withdrawal only about 20 percent of the time, the kinds of situations where withdrawal was a likely means of coping were different for the two groups. German adolescents indicated withdrawal behavior twice as often as the Israelis when the problems involved the "self" or "leisure time." German adolescents preferred active coping styles over half the time when it came to problems dealing with "parents" and "the opposite sex," compared with only about a third of the time for the Israelis. This was the greatest cultural difference between the two groups.

Incidentally, researchers found gender differences among both groups. Both German and Israeli girls chose active support-seeking more than the boys, but German girls were more likely than boys to use withdrawal as a coping mechanism.

Why did Germans make greater use of active strategies while the Israelis prefered internal coping processes? An explanation for this might be found in each culture's history. The history of the Jews and of Israel has been one of rejection, persecution, and ghettoization. These are all conditions that could foster a people's self-reliance. German youths, on the other hand, live in a society that has a long history of stressing the importance of deference to authority figures.

Thus, culture does seem to create social differences in how people try to solve their problems. Although Germans and Israelis demonstrated many similar responses to coping, factors that involve their cultural history apparently influenced their coping styles.

■ References

Seiffge-Krenke, I., & Schulman, S. (1990). Coping style in adolescence: A cross-cultural study. *Journal of Cross-Cultural Psychology*, *21*, 351-377.

■ Discussion Questions

1. Describe and give an example of the three coping strategies used by adolescents.

2. How do German and Israeli youths differ in their approach to solving problems? (Be specific.)

3. What gender differences were there in coping styles?

4.   What other historical cultural factors might influence how a group
     of people reacts to stress? How similar are American adolescents to
     these two groups studied by Seiffge-Krenke and Shulman?

■ For Further Exploration

1.   Discuss the pros and cons of defining withdrawal as a healthy style
     of coping. Is withdrawal inherently dysfunctional?

■ For Additional Reading

Lazarus, R. S. (1976). *Pattern of adjustment*. New York: McGraw-Hill.
     Discusses coping and how it differs from defense.

McCubbin, H. J., Cauble, A. E., & Patterson, J. M. (1982). *Family
     stress, coping, and social support*. Springfield, IL: Charles C.
     Thomas. Examines the role of family in the development of coping
     styles.

"Call Me Crazy"!
Psychiatric Labeling Among the
Eskimo and the Yoruba

■ Stimulus Questions

Are the labeling and stigmatization of "mental disorder" phenomena particular to Western society? Or do other societies have concepts of mental disorders that parallel our own?

PSYCHIATRIST Thomas Szasz (1970) has argued that all concepts of mental disorders are really nothing more than societal value judgments about people's behavior clothed in the objective-sounding language of science. That is, although Western psychiatry's traditional language of "mental illness," "psychodiagnosis," and "treatment" in "mental hospitals" implies that we are practicing a form of medicine, all evaluations about a person's mental functioning are value judgments about behavior. And behavior is normal or abnormal because it conforms or deviates from cultural rules about what is acceptable or unacceptable. Thus, "mental illness" doesn't really exist in the same sense that tuberculosis or cancer exists. Thomas Scheff (1984), a well-known sociologist, developed an entire approach to mental disorders based on a related idea—that people who deviate from socially approved behavior are labeled "crazy" by other members of society to preserve the stability of that society. At one time R. D. Laing (1967), a British psychiatrist, even interpreted mental disorders as extreme as schizo-

phrenia as "normal" psychological processes that help individuals cope
with particular kinds of stress.

The existence of ethnic disorder such as *kayak-angst* among the
Greenland Eskimo and *koro* in southern China also suggests that there
can be tremendous cultural differences in mental disorders and their
symptoms. But does this mean that if we accept the Western idea of
mental disorders we are merely engaging in a form of cultural prejudice?
Are we falsely assuming that our own Western values about how people
ought to behave are universally valid psychological "disorders?" Jane
Murphy (1976), an anthropologist, has considered this question by
examining the concepts of psychological disorders that are found in two
distinctly non-Western cultures and comparing them with our own. She
found that both the Yapic-speaking Eskimo who occupy an island in the
Bering Sea, and the Yoruba, an agricultural group from Nigeria, West
Africa, had ideas on this subject that are very close to our own. Murphy
believes that this supports the claim that mental disorders do objectively
exist. She concludes that the concept of mental disorders is not merely
an expression of Western values, but represents a basic human way of
perceiving some behavior as evidence of abnormal psychological
processes.

Both the Eskimo and the Yoruba distinguish between the body and
the mind and have terms for mental disorders, or at least clusters of
behaviors, that they consider abnormal. Like Americans, the Eskimo
have a word that means "crazy," *nathkavihak*, which to the Eskimo
implies that a person's mind or soul is out of order. Such people may talk
to themselves, scream at nonexistent persons, or claim that a child or
husband was murdered by witchcraft when nobody else believes it. They
may say they are animals, or refuse to eat for fear that they will die from
the food, or may refuse to talk. Sometimes they run away from others,
get lost, hide in strange places, make strange grimaces, drink urine,
become unusually strong and violent, kill dogs, or threaten other people
(p. 1022). The Yoruba have similar ideas about mental disorders. Their
word for the same kinds of abnormal behaviors, *were*, means about the
same as the colloquial English word "insanity."

Both the Eskimo and the Yoruba distinguish individual symptoms
from true psychological disorders. For instance, just hearing voices is
not enough to get someone labeled *nathkavihak* or *were*. It is only when
such a claim is part of a larger cluster of three or four other unusual
behaviors, such as paranoid fears and hostile behaviors towards others,
that it indicates an abnormal mental condition. This view of mental
disorders as clusters of symptoms is like that followed by DSM-III-R,
the current diagnostic manual of the American Psychiatric Association.

An interesting fact about both the Eskimo and the Yoruba is that, like Americans, they distinguish true mental disorders from certain other phenomena. Both the Eskimo and the Yoruba distinguish between people who are mentally disturbed and others who have special abilities. For instance, their religious curers hear voices, see into the future, or become possessed by animal spirits. But they never use the words *were* and *nathkavihak* to describe these religious leaders. Like most Americans, who do not consider a religious leader to be suffering from a mental disorder for claiming to have received answers to prayers, the Yoruba and Eskimo recognize that a religious curer who hears voices during a trance will behave normally at other times. The Eskimo, the Yoruba, and the Americans, all note the same difference between the truly mentally ill and others who sometimes express extraordinary ideas or behave in unusual ways. They think of someone as having a mental disorder if he or she doesn't seem to be in control of their unusual behavior. Religious leaders may occasionally enter states of religious rapture that have similarities to individual symptoms of a mental disorder. But these are only a temporary state from which they are expected to be able to return. They may "go out of their minds" on such special occasions, but they have not "lost their minds." Only those who seem to have lost control over their unusual behaviors are thought of as "crazy" in America or in other cultures.

Murphy noted that some Western psychiatric categories had no specific labels among the Yoruba and the Eskimo. For example, the Yoruba have no term equivalent to senility. There are certainly some very old Yoruba who cannot take care of themselves, who wander about and talk to themselves, but there was no explicit label for this condition. Similarly, no term exists among either the Eskimo or Yoruba for anxiety or depression, but there were terms for the individual symptoms that American diagnosticians normally associate with depression or anxiety. For example, the Yoruba have specific words that refer to "the unrest of the mind that prevents sleep" or "the fear of being among people." And the Eskimo can describe conditions such as "too easy to get afraid" or "crying with sadness" or "trembling all over." So although an overall classification didn't exist for an anxiety disorder or for depression, this did not imply that the Eskimo and Yoruba were unaware of the problems that these disorders represent. In fact, they thought of these individual symptoms as illnesses and believed that they required treatment by religious curers. According to Murphy, such problems as these were much more common than were the formally labeled mental disorders of *were* and *nathkavihak*. She estimated that there was about a 12 to 1 ratio between those who suffered from depressive and anxiety disorders versus those who were called "crazy" among the Yoruba. Among the Eskimo, the ratio was about 14 to 1. This parallels the higher frequency of disorders such as depression and anxiety compared with schizophrenia, the Western disorder that is equivalent to *were* or *nathkavihak*.

Both the Eskimo and the Yoruba have words for various forms of "bad conduct" that contrast with mental disorders. They have words that describe cheating, lying, theft, drunkenness, and stinginess. The Eskimo use the word *kunlangeta* to describe a person whose mind knows what to do but he does not do it. The Yoruba use the word *arankan* to express a very similar condition. A person who is called *arankan* is always out for himself and is rarely cooperative and perhaps full of malice. Similar people in the West, who violate societal norms, might be diagnosed as suffering from a personality disorder. People who demonstrate such antisocial behavior are not believed to be treatable by Eskimo or Yoruba religious curers. This is not so different from the views of American psychotherapists, who generally regard personality disorders as being among the least treatable psychiatric conditions.

A number of researchers have collected information about the incidence of schizophrenia around the world. Studies done in Europe, North America, and Asia indicate that the prevalence of this disorder is quite comparable everywhere. Certainly, cultural variations do exist, but the proportion of people exhibiting characteristics of schizophrenia is very consistent. Murphy compared the prevalence rates of *were* and *nathkavihak* with the rates of schizophrenia in Sweden and Canada. Proportionally she found no major differences in the rates of these disorders in the four cultures. Like schizophrenia, *were* and *nathkavihak* were relatively rare. Among the Yoruba in 1961 only 2 cases of *were* were identified. The proportion of the entire Yoruba population that this represented was about the same as the proportion of diagnosed schizophrenics that Murphy found in the Swedish population. Murphy estimated a total presence for all forms of "mental illness" in three of these cultures where she had done personal research and judged them to be quite comparable: Canada, 18%; Eskimo, 19%; and Yoruba, 15%.

Because of her comparative findings, Murphy claims that living in a non-Western culture does not seem to provide any particular insulation against mental disorders. There are cultural differences in the particular symptoms of each disorder; however, mental disorders occur in all cultures. The specific symptoms may differ, but the general qualities of what we call mental disorders seem to be the same, as does their prevalence. Moreover, all cultures appear to label some specific behaviors in a way that is similar to the categories and definitions used by Western psychiatry. And even though some Western mental disorders may not have a single term to describe them in some other cultures, the disorders are recognized in those societies and their symptoms seem to be regarded as problems that require treatment.

■ References

Laing, R. D. (1967). *The politics of experience*. New York: Random House.

Murphy, J. M. (1976). Psychiatric labeling in cross-cultural perspective. *Science, 191*, 1019-1028.

Scheff, T. (1984). *Being mentally ill: A sociological theory* (2nd ed.). Chicago: Aldine.

Szasz, T. S. (1970). *Ideology and insanity: Essays on the psychiatric dehumanization of man*. New York: Doubleday.

■ Discussion Questions

1. How do non-Western societies differ from Western ones in their concepts of mental disorders?

2. Why are religious curers *not* classified as having *were* or *nathkavihak*?

■ For Further Exploration

1. How do the characteristics of schizophrenia as described in the DSM-III-R compare to those symptoms describing the Eskimo condition of *nathkavihak*?

2. Some claim that psychodiagnosis is really a value judgment about people's behavior (and therefore fundamentally different from a medical diagnosis about a disease). Others argue that there are universally valid categories of abnormal behavior that can be objectively determined to exist. Discuss ways of reconciling these two viewpoints about mental disorders.

■ For Additional Reading

Foulks, E. F. (1972). *The Arctic hysterias of the North Alaskan Eskimo.* Washington, D.C.: American Anthropological Association. Summarizes the various forms of anxiety disorders and hysterical disorders that have been reported among the northern Alaskan Eskimo and discusses their possible causes.

Depression and Culture

■ Stimulus Questions

Does depression exist in some cultures but not in others? How might a cultural group's view of the world color its acceptance of depressive symptoms (as defined from a Western point of view) as normal, or even good?

MOOD disorders such as depression have a long history in Western societies. As early as the fifth century B.C., Hippocrates described the symptoms of melancholia as "aversion to food, despondency, sleeplessness, irritability, restlessness" (Jones & Withington, 1923). Today, the American Psychiatric Association (1994) lists as criteria for the diagnosis of a "major depressive episode" the presence for at least a two-week period of at least five of the following symptoms: depressed mood nearly every day (or irritability in children), loss of interest or pleasure in most activities, nonplanned loss or gain of appetite or weight, insomnia or hypersomnia, observable agitation or slowing of movement, daily fatigue, subjective feelings of worthlessness or guilt, loss of ability to think or concentrate, and recurrent thoughts of death or suicide.

In the United States untreated episodes typically last about six months, and from 10 to 25% of women and from 5 to 12% of men experience two such episodes during their lives. But rates of depression vary tremendously from culture to culture. For instance, Manson, Shore, and Bloom (1985) have reported that rates of depression in Native American communities may be up to six times as high as for the rest of the United States. On the other hand, many reports have suggested that the cluster of symptoms thought of as depression in Western psychology may be uncommon in most non-Western cultures. Various researchers have denied the presence of native concepts of depression among groups as diverse as Nigerians (Leighton, Lambe, Hughes, Leighton, Murphy, & Macklin, 1963), Chinese (Tseng & Hsu, 1969), Canadian Inuit (Terminsen & Ryan, 1970), Japanese (Tanaka-Matsumi & Marsella, 1976), and Malaysians (Resner & Hartog, 1970).

Manson et al. (1985) did a careful study of Hopi concepts of mental disorders that have symptoms found in Western psychiatric definitions of depression. They found that the Hopi have no disorder that corresponds to the Western concept of depression, but instead distinguish between five separate illnesses that have some depressive symptoms: worry sickness, unhappiness, heartbreak, drunkenlike craziness (with or without alcohol), and disappointment-pouting. Each of these is defined by its own distinctive cluster of symptoms, and each is treated with a different Hopi therapy. A Western patient who has been diagnosed as suffering from "depression" would have to be rediagnosed as having one of the five Hopi conditions before treatment could be prescribed. From the Hopi perspective, the Western psychiatric category of depression is much too general and vague to be therapeutically useful.

Murphy, Wittkower, and Chance (1964) surveyed thirty countries for symptoms of depression. In twenty-one of them the symptoms of depressed mood, diurnal variation, insomnia, and loss of interest in the environment were noted, but in nine countries, most of which were non-Western, the common symptoms were somatic ones such as fatigue, anorexia, weight loss, and loss of libido. Such findings were still common twenty years later. Furthermore, Kleinman (1986) noted less guilt and less low self-esteem among depressed Chinese, and similar reports have been given of Filipinos (Sechrest, 1963), and the Senegalese (German, 1972).

A possible explanation for the relative absence of symptoms, such as self-blame, guilt, and feelings of worthlessness, may relate to how people in other cultures are socialized in different ways to interpret their feelings. For instance, El-Islam (1969) has suggested that guilt is commonly replaced by blaming others in many non-Western cultures. A study by Edward Schieffelin (1985) provides an interesting illustration of this idea. Schieffelin studied the Kaluli people, who occupy the tropical forest north of Mount Bosavi in Papua, New Guinea. The Kaluli way of life includes no governing officials such as chiefs. Communities are based on the interaction of equals, but individuals may rise or fall in prestige and public influence through their own efforts. Assertiveness is highly valued among the Kaluli, who are socialized to be energetic in support of their friends. In seeking personal advantage in public life, the support of friends is needed. Lack of assertiveness and initiative are stigmatized.

The Kaluli are not socialized to suppress their feelings. For the Kaluli, part of assertiveness in public life is the willingness of a man to express anger towards those who interfere with his goals. Similarly, Kaluli men are equally willing to express emotions such as grief and dismay or to elicit compassion and support from friends. Thus the Kaluli individual readily expresses both anger and grief in response to frustration or loss as a means to assert rights, or to seek redress, over whomever the Kaluli holds responsible. The pattern of showing emotion in order to communicate one's sense of having been wronged holds for both men and women, although the public expression of emotion is more dramatic among the men. The customary expression of feelings in public settings draws children into the same pattern of channeling emotions.

Schieffelin contends that Kaluli social life, which encourages the Kaluli to mobilize their anger or grief in service of their demands for recompense from those who have wronged them, makes it unlikely for the Kaluli to experience depression in the Western sense of "aggression-turned-inward". According to Schieffelin, "Kaluli do not blame themselves over their misfortunes in life; anger and blame over loss or disappointment are always turned outward according to the view of reciprocity as a sense of feeling wronged and owed rather than as a sense of inward blame, guilt, or self-hate. Similarly, for views such as the one that holds that depression results from an unresolved grief experience in childhood . . . Kaluli cultural modalities for dealing with grief and anger would seem to minimize the possibilities of this and related factors being the basis of Kaluli depression" (p. 115).

In a society in which it is normal to blame others rather than one's self for life's failures, it is not surprising that the Kaluli language has no word for depression. But does this mean that the Kaluli do not experience something that could be recognized as a form of depression by the standards of Western psychology? Schieffelin suggests that, if depression occurred among the Kaluli, it would most likely be expressed through somatic symptoms such as headaches, stomach disorders, low energy, and subdued social behavior. The situations which might precipitate diagnosable depression would also be unusual, since Kaluli custom encouraged people to direct their internal stresses outward as complaints against others. Somatic forms of depression, manifested as bodily aches and pains, would be most likely in a situation in which personal frustrations were caused by circumstances in which complaints against others were considered not legitimate.

After four years of observation, Schieffelin was able to point to only one example of a person whom he believed might be experiencing major depression. The case he cites is a bright, lively young woman who was required, against her own wishes, to become the third wife of a powerful man who was known to beat his wives. By Kaluli custom, she could not protest this marriage. Happiness—though desirable—is not a reason for marriage among the Kaluli. Marriage is more than a union of the husband and wife. It links their respective families and their communities in a social and political alliance. Divorce is difficult and requires the cooperation of the husband and of the wife's relatives, who may have a vested interest in the continuation of the marriage. In the case cited by Schieffelin, the marriage had been arranged by the woman's brother as part of an agreement allowing him to marry the sister of the man his own sister married. This meant that if she did leave her husband, her own brother's marriage would have to be ended. So she was effectively trapped in a marriage she could not accept or complain against. According to Schieffelin, "After a little more than a year of marriage she had lost her sparkle. While she continued to perform wifely duties, she had become markedly subdued and seemed inattentive and distracted in social interactions. She complained of a constant headache, which she said she had had for over a year. Both she and others recognized that she was not herself. On two occasions she had consulted a mission doctor about her physical complaints, but he had not been able to determine what was wrong with her" (p. 118).

Gananeth Obeyesekere (1985) raised the issue of whether the ideology of a culture might make depression an undiagnosable condition. He considered the common Western definition of depression as a response to loss that includes symptoms such as hopelessness, distress, shame, and anger. His reaction was that such a description ". . . sounds strange to me, a Buddhist, for if it was placed in the context of Sri Lanka, I would say that we are not dealing with a depressive but a good Buddhist" (p. 134). To the Sri Lankan Buddhist, "hopelessness lies in the nature of the world, the salvation lies in understanding and overcoming that hopelessness" (p. 134) The Sri Lankan Buddhist ideology "states that life is suffering and sorrow, that the cause of sorrow is attachment or desire or craving, that there is a way (generally through meditation) of understanding and overcoming suffering and achieving the final goal of cessation for suffering" (p. 134). In a society in which such views of suffering as a normal state were widely shared, the idea of diagnosing depression as a pathological condition within an individual would not make sense. Obeyesekere recounts a personal experience that illustrates this point. "A colleague of mine, a clinical psychologist from the United States, visited me in Sri Lanka many years ago. I introduced him to a friend of mine and the two of them got to know each other well. Before my colleague left for the United States, he told me: 'Gananeth, your friend is a classic case of depression.' I was somewhat startled, for though my friend had a sad expression and a pessimistic view of the world, I never thought of him in quite that way. My friend did not regard himself as a depressive. Neither his wife nor his physicians considered him one. My friend was a manager of a government corporation, but often used to get away from it all . . . by going to meditate in isolated hermitages . . . His was neither a disease nor an illness; he had generalized his hopelessness into an ontological problem of existence, defined in its Buddhist sense as 'suffering'" (p. 139). Is the Sri Lankan case unique? Both the Ashanti (Africa) and the Yoruba (Africa) are further examples of cultures with an idcology that might make the diagnosis of depression a moot point. According to Kraus (1968), " There is a high incidence of involutional psychotic reactions of thc depressed type among Ashanti women. This type of depression seems, in fact, not to be thought of as an illness but accepted as the inevitable lot of most women" (p. 25). Among the Yoruba, "Depression presented a special problem in that while the symptoms were recognized as painful, unpleasant and disabling, they were seen as more or less 'natural' results of the vicissitudes of life" (p. 26).

Obeyesekere's point is not that sadness and grief, difficulty in concentrating, and other experiences that are defined as symptoms of depression in Western psychology are absent in some cultures, but that the nature of culture makes it unlikely that such experiences would be perceived as diagnosable "disorders". This amounts to more than simply claiming that depression exists in these cultures but is simply not perceived as such. Obeyesekere's point is that the practice of isolating symptoms from their cultural context in order to treat them as part of a diseaselike condition containts a hidden flaw. If depression, as currently defined in Western culture and psychiatric diagnosis, is not found in non-Western cultures, how do we know that "depression" is not merely a Western folk-concept analogous to other culture-specific conditions, such as koro, kayak angst, amok, or susto?

■ References

American Psychiatric Association. (1994). *Diagnostic and statistical manual of mental disorders* (4th ed.). Washington, D.C.: Author.

El-Islam, F. (1969). Depression and guilt: A study at an Arab psychiatric center. *Social Psychiatry, 4*, 56-58.

German, A. (1972). Aspects of clinical psychiatry in Sub-Saharan Africa. *British Journal of Psychiatry, 121*, 461-470.

Jones, W.H.S., & Withington, E.T. (Trans. and Eds.). (1923). *Works of Hippocrates* (Vol. 1). Cambridge, MA: Harvard University Press.

Kleinman, A. (1986). *Social origins of distress and disease: Depression, Neurasthenia, and pain in modern China.* New Haven, CT: Yale University Press.

Leighton, A., Lambe, T., Hughes, C., Leighton, D., Murphy, J., & Macklin, A.M. (1963). *Psychiatric disorders among the Yoruba.* Ithaca, NY: Cornell University Press.

Krause, R.F. (1968). Cross-cultural validation of psychoanalytic theories of depression. *Pennsylvania Psychiatric Quarterly, 3*(8), 24-33.

Manson S., Shore J., & Bloom, J. (1985). The depressive experience in American Indian communities: A challenge for psychiatric theory and diagnosis. In A. Kleinman and B. Good (Eds.), *Culture and depression.* Berkeley: University of California Press.

Murphy, H., Wittkower, E., & Chance, N. (1964). Cross-cultural inquiry into the symptomatology of depression. *Transcultural Psychiatric Research Review, 1*, 5-21.

Obeyesekere, G. (1985). Depression, Buddhism, and the work of culture in Sri Lanka. In A. Kleinman and B. Good (Eds.), *Culture and depression.* Berkeley: University of California Press.

Resner, G., & Hartog, J. (1970). Concepts and terminology of mental disorders among Malays. *Journal of Cross-Cultural Psychology, 1*, 369-381.

Schieffelin, L. (1985). The cultural analysis of depressive affect: An example of New Guinea. In A. Kleinman and B. Good (Eds.), *Culture and depression.* Berkeley: University of California Press.

Sechrest, L. (1963). Symptoms of mental disorder in the Philippines. *Philippine Sociological Review, 7*, 189-206.

Tanaka-Matsumi, J., & Marsella, A.J. (1976). Cross-cultural variations in the phenomenological experience of depression: Word association. *Journal of Cross-Cultural Psychology, 7*, 33-39.

Terminsen, J., & Ryan, J. (1970). Health and disease in a British Columbia community. *Canadian Psychiatric Association Journal, 15*, 121-127.

Tseng, W., & Hsu, J. (1969). Chinese culture, personality formation and mental illness. *International Journal of Social Psychiatry, 16*, 5-14.

■ Discussion Questions

1. What socialization processes and social behaviors do the Kaluli of Papua New Guinea engage in which make them less susceptible to the Western notion of depression?

2. Obeyesekere suggests that a culture's ideology may determine whether or not depression is diagnosable. How does the Sri Lankan Buddhist example illustrate this point?

3. In your opinion, is the Western definition of depression flawed, or are the different patterns of this disorder simply different expressions of the same condition?

■ For Additional Reading

Kleinman, A. (1990). *Psychosocial aspects of depression*. Hillsdale, NJ: Lawrence Erlbaum.

Kleinman, A. (1988). *Rethinking psychiatry*. New York: Free Press.

Kleinman, A., & Good, B. (Eds.). (1985). *Culture and depression*. Berkeley: University of California Press.

Koro—A Culture-Bound Depersonalization Syndrome

■ Stimulus Question

Can a particular cultural belief or expectation bring on a psychiatric disorder?

DEPERSONALIZATION is an experience in which people feel a sudden sense of unreality and strangeness about themselves. They may even feel that their body has drastically changed, perhaps in some grotesque fashion. Depersonalization experiences are relatively common in our society. They generally result from an episode of acute stress. Mild forms of so-called out-of-body experiences fall within the category of dissociative disorders.

In various parts of the world, there are variations of disorders that include a type of depersonalization that substantially differs from that typically found in the West. For example, several anxiety syndromes exist that entail intense fear of death, castration anxiety, and concern about male sexuality. The Yoruba of Nigeria believe that "bewitchment" can cause sexual difficulties such as male impotence. They believe a male witch can take another man's penis and return it after using it to have intercourse with the victim's wife or with some other woman. This leaves the penis in an altered and impotent form (Kiev, 1972, p. 70).

Koro is a southern Chinese anxiety disorder that includes depersonalization with an emphasis on fears of sexual dysfunction and death (Hsien, 1963; Yap, 1965). Victims of koro worry compulsively over what they view as sexual excess. They also lack confidence in their own sexual capacity and thus their sense of virility. This sexual anxiety leads to the body-image distortion syndrome that accompanies depersonalization.

The victim of *koro* suffers from the delusion that his penis is shrinking and retracting into his abdomen, and that he will die when the process is complete. Another name for koro is *suk-yeong*, which means shrinkage of the penis (Yap, 1964). Koro appears to affect younger Chinese males (21 to 40 years of age) who have a sexual history of conflict or maladjustment. Guilt and anxiety arise out of real or imagined sexual excess, especially autoerotic activity, causing a panic-like state. These young men lack confidence in their own virility. Yap describes most of them as being immature, relatively unintelligent, and dependent. Most live in the lower Yang-tse valley. However, cases of the disorder have also been reported in Malaysia and Indonesia. As far back as 700 years ago in China, people believed that health was the result of an equilibrium between the "yang" (male) and the "yin" (female) humours. During masturbation or nocturnal emissions, an unhealthy loss of "yang" took place putting the individual in an unbalanced condition.

Most episodes of koro occur at night. Symptoms accompanying the anxiety include faintness, a feeling of impending death, palpitation, trembling, and even a tingling in the genital area. So strong is this depersonalization anxiety that a number of men believed they must hold on to their penis all during an attack so that it would not disappear by shrinking inside them. The need to visually inspect and touch their genitals is paramount to confirm their size and existence. Hsien (1965) describes the following individual:

> Almost irresistible sexual desire seized him whenever he felt slightly better; yet he experienced strange "empty" feelings in his abdomen when he had sexual intercourse. He reported that he often found his penis shrinking into his abdomen, at which time he would become very anxious and hold his penis in terror. Holding his penis, he would faint, with severe vertigo and pounding of his heart. For four months he drank a cup of *torn-biann* (boys's urine) each morning, and this helped him a great deal. He also thought that his anus was withdrawing into his abdomen every other day or so. At night he would find that his penis had shrunk to a length of only one centimeter and he would pull it out and then be able to relax and go to sleep. (p. 8)

Basic Chinese folk culture may give some clues to the causes of Koro (Hsien, 1965). In Malay the word *koro* means the head of the turtle. For many years the Chinese used the symbol of the turtle to stand for longevity and the vital forces within a person. There is also the obvious resemblance between the head of the long-lived tortoise and the glans penis. According to Yap (1964), fears about nocturnal emissions, impotence, and general debility helped generate the belief of koro. These fears grew out of the interaction between (a) practices concerned with sexual hygiene and adequate sexual performance, and (b) traditional Chinese beliefs about how the balance of yang and yin humours affected people's physical and sexual health.

A combination of psychological, social and cultural factors predisposes an individual to the body-image distortion of koro. Since this disorder is connected to Chinese concepts of sexuality, Kiev (1972) has suggested that one factor in a predisposition to koro may be an immature, dependent nature caused by unresolved Oedipal conflicts. Cultural beliefs in koro as a manifestation of loss of masculine yang essence can also predispose a person who feels guilt over sexual excess—especially guilt about masturbation—into a full-blown attack of koro anxiety.

Cultural concepts about koro magnify its psychological effect on individuals who suffer from it. For instance, in Chinese folk belief the koro illness is dangerous and one may die because of it. The fears that this belief generates can leave a person who experiences sexual anxiety that they associate with koro feeling helpless and panic-stricken.

Koro is unlike other states of depersonalization in which a person might realize that they are simply "spaced-out" because of stress. The person with koro has only limited insight into his condition. Yet he does not suffer more wide-spread emotional disturbances. Thus, koro is a distinctive condition, a "culture-bound" condition or "ethnic disorder" specific to the Chinese culture.

Nevertheless, some of the elements of koro have definite parallels in other cultures. Carstairs (1956) found a psychological disturbance among Hindu men that includes ideas like the yin-yang concept of China connected to the belief that losing semen is dangerous to a man's health. Nineteenth-century Victorian beliefs involved similar concepts. Medical doctors of that day taught that overindulgence in sex or masturbation would lead to debilitation and even insanity. That such ideas did not develop into a formal recognized psychiatric disorder in Euro-American cultures is perhaps only a matter of historical accident.

■ References

Carstairs, G. M. (1956). Hinjra and Jiran. *British Journal of Medical Psychology*, *19*, 128.

Hsien, R. (1963). A consideration on Chinese concepts of illness and case illustrations. *Transcultural Psychiatry Research*, *15*, 23-30.

Hsien, R. (1965). A study of the aetiology of koro in respect to the Chinese concept of illness. *International Journal of Social Psychiatry*, *2*, 7-13.

Kiev, A. (1972). *Transcultural psychiatry*. New York: The Free Press.

Yap, P. M. (1964). Suk-yeong or koro–A culture-bound depersonalization syndrome. *The Bulletin of the Hong Kong Medical Association*, *16*, 1, 31-47.

Yap, P. M. (1965). Koro–A culture-bound depersonalization syndrome. *British Journal of Psychiatry*, *111*, 43-50.

■ Discussion Questions

1. Why has koro been classified as an anxiety-type disorder?

2. What characteristics of Chinese culture may make it difficult for victims of koro to have much insight into the unreality of their depersonalization experience?

3. What individual characteristics may predispose southern Chinese men to the experience of koro?

■ For Further Exploration

1. At the foundation of the koro syndrome are both sexual anxieties and cultural beliefs. Find examples of psychosexual dysfunctions that might be termed typically Western. What are the causes of these disorders?

2. Other culture-bound disorders have been identified around the world: *susto* (Spanish-American); *shinkeishitu* (Japanese); *latah* or *imu* (Japanese); *mal ojo* (Mexican-American); *hiwa:itck* (Mohave Indian); *muyu-muyu* (Quechua); voodoo death (widespread); *negi-negi* (African); *amok* (Malaysian); *hsieh-ping* (Chinese); *boufée delirante aigüe* (Haitian) and *pibloktoq* (Eskimo). Find an article related to one of these psychiatric conditions for an oral or written report.

■ For Additional Reading

Simons, R. C., & Hughes, C. C. (1985). *The culture-bound syndromes: Folk illnesses of psychiatric and anthropological interest*. Boston: D. Reidel. Describes a variety of culture-bound mental disorders and analyzes them in terms of contemporary Western psychiatric classification.

Gimme A Break!
Patterns of Cooperation
Among Mexican Americans,
African Americans, and
Anglo-Americans

■ Stimulus Questions

To what degree is competition among individuals a culturally determined phenomenon? Are people naturally competitive? Would Americans be less competitive if their social conditions were different?

STOP ARGUING! Why can't you kids ever seem to get along with each other?" It is an altogether too familiar phrase heard in households across the United States. We Americans long for the cooperative family life of Ozzie and Harriet and the Waltons, but our real experience even makes Married With Children seem like harmless fun and games. Psychologists and anthropologists have asked whether the American emphasis on individualism and competition may be partly to blame for the lack of cooperation that so often typifies our society. Certain other cultures provide a marked contrast. Consider the the Zuñi of Arizona. According to Ruth Benedict (1934), they emphasized conformity and cooperation to the point that they did not even encourage their children to excel over their peers. Rather, they prompted them to give other children a chance to win. Their religious customs included no spontaneous personal prayers but consisted solely of recitation of traditional prayers. Benedict describes Zuñi dance in similar terms: "The dance, like their ritual poetry, is a monotonous compulsion of natural forces by reiteration. . . . There is nothing wild about them. It is the cumulative force of the rhythm, the perfection of forty men moving as one, that makes them effective" (pp. 92-93).

The Zuñi chose their political leaders very differently from how Americans do. They never chose the outstanding individual who proved his superiority over other candidates with glib answers to every question. The ideal Zuñi candidate would never have shown such pride and competitiveness but instead would have tried to convince others that there were better choices available for public office. Indeed, the Zuñi so opposed competitiveness that their only role model for competitive individualism and striving to rise above the common herd was the witch, the embodiment of evil. The Zuñi witch's demeanor was a lot like that of some U.S. politicians and competitive young executives—proud and self-confident. The Zuñi dealt harshly with those whom they suspected of being witches. They killed them. So the Zuñi grew up knowing that they should take seriously the ideals of noncompetitive cooperativeness. They didn't just dream about such ideals with nostalgia, the way Americans do today when they watch unrealistically loving soap opera families unwind after a hard day of competitive infighting.

Anthropologists and psychologists have evaluated the influences of a number of different factors to understand why cultures and sub-cultures (local variants of the mainstream culture) differ in the cooperative and competitive behavior they encourage. They have also examined how cooperativeness and competitiveness differ by age and gender. And, of course, they look at how the expectation of reward for cooperation or competition affects the performance of individuals, since people will often violate their culture's ideals for a desired reward.

One consistent finding has been that urban individuals in many different societies demonstrate greater competitiveness than people from a small town or rural environment. Anthropological studies offer various explanations for this phenomenon. For instance, small town dwellers may fear ostracism for being competitive—a significant punishment when success depends on acceptance by your neighbors. Religious beliefs support cooperation within the community more effectively when the neighborhood is the same group people worship with. And cooperative behavior pays off in rural life, since those who help their neighbors are more likely to be helped by others when they are in need.

In 1970 Madsen and Shapira looked for subcultural differences among Afro-, Anglo-, and Mexican-American children seven to nine years of age. They found few significant differences among these groups when it came to cooperative versus competitive behavior. When groups were rewarded for successful cooperation, children in these three groups were equally cooperative. But once they introduced the alternative of individual reward, the children of all three groups became much more competitive and less cooperative, particularly the Afro and Anglo-

Americans. However, the subcultural differences among these three American groups were less than the differences between kibbutz and nonkibbutz children in Israel (Shapira & Madsen, 1969) or village and urban children in Mexico (Spiro, 1965).

Madsen and Shapira also wondered whether these samples of ethnic Americans would differ greatly from a sample of children from a rural, village area outside the United States. The answer was yes. Village children in Mexico differed significantly from the three American groups in that they were as prone to show cooperative behavior as the ethnic American children were to display competitiveness. The American children often engaged in aggressive, wild, shouting matches to win a game. Their behavior was so competitive that it even interfered with the goal of winning prizes when cooperation was necessary. The rural Mexican children were more successful in gaining these rewards for cooperative behavior. The rural-urban contrast that distinguished American urban children from Mexican rural children also showed up within Mexico itself. Madsen and Shapira (1970) found that urban Mexican children were just as competitive as the Afro-, Anglo-, and Mexican-American children.

Kagan and Madsen (1971) obtained similar results in later experiments with Anglo-, Mexican-American, and Mexican children in which they looked for age differences in cooperation and competition. They found that younger children (ages 4 to 5) were more cooperative with one another than older children (ages 7 to 9) when asked to play certain games. Interestingly, the increase in competitiveness showed up in the group that had just entered what Erikson called the developmental stage of "industry versus inferiority," a period where children either learn to be personally competent and effective at activities valued by adults or begin to feel inferior. This development of a strong, self-willed "I" orientation began near age seven for both Anglo- and Mexican Americans and led to irrational, competitive strategies even when cooperative behavior was more rewarded.

Mexican cultural values of cooperativeness provided some insulation against the rise of competitive self-centeredness in the Mexican children, who were less competitive than either Anglo-American or Mexican-American children in all the tests. The Anglo-American children consistently turned out to be the most competitive in these studies, and the Mexican-American children were always intermediate between the Mexican children and the Anglo-Americans. In other words, the game strategies of the Mexican-American children seemed to show influences of both of their cultural heritages.

References

Benedict, R. (1934). *Patterns of culture*. Boston: Houghton Mifflin.

Kagan, S., & Madsen, M. C. (1971). Cooperation and competition of Mexican, Mexican-American, and Anglo-American children of two ages under four instructional sets. *Developmental Psychology, 5,* 32-39.

Madsen, M.C., & Shapira, A. (1970). Cooperative and competitive behavior of urban Afro-American, Anglo-American, Mexican-American, and Mexican village children. *Developmental Psychology, 3,* 16-20.

Shapira, A., & Madsen, M. C. (1969). Cooperative and competitive behavior of kibbutz and urban children in Israel. *Child Development, 40,* 609-617.

Spiro, M. E. (1965). *Children of the Kibbutz*. Cambridge, MA: Harvard University Press.

Discussion Questions

1. What evidence exists to support the idea that cooperative-competitive behavior is influenced by the cultural environment in which one lives?

2. Why could the competitive orientation of Anglo-American children be considered maladaptive?

3. What are the explanations for differences in cooperative behaviors of various cultural groups?

For Further Exploration

1. Using an experimental game board similar to that devised by Kagan and Madsen (see their 1971 article for rules and instructions), replicate their experiment with children at a local pre-school and elementary school. How do your subjects compare?

For Additional Reading

Hsu, F. L. K. (1961). *Chinese and Americans: A study of two cultures*. New York: Henry Schuman. An analytic comparison of Chinese and American culture with emphasis on the contrasting roles of competitive individualism and cooperation and interdependence.

Hsu, F. L. K. (1983). *Rugged individualism reconsidered: Essays in psychological anthropology*. Knoxville, TN: University of Tennessee Press. A collection of articles by a Chinese anthropologist, each of which examines aspects of American competitive individualism, a hallmark of American culture.

Polyandry—Multiple Spouses in Tibet and Pahari, India

■ Stimulus Questions

From a sociological point of view, what advantages or consequences would there be for two or more brothers to marry the same woman? What tensions might develop between brothers in such a relationship?

IT is rare for a woman to have several husbands. Probably fewer than 0.5 percent of human societies have practiced this form of marriage, called *polyandry*, as a common or preferred form of marriage. But throughout Tibet and the neighboring Himalayan areas of India, Nepal, and Bhutan, polyandry has been common for generations. In this area a polyandrous marriage is usually one in which a woman marries two or more brothers. Like other polyandrous societies, the people of this region do not limit themselves strictly to polyandry (Levine & Sangree, 1980). Their communities include families that are monogamous, polygamous, and polyandrous. Some families even unite several husbands and several wives into "group marriages."

Goldstein (1979) has examined polyandry in two different Himalayan regions—the Limi Valley in northwest Nepal, and Pahari, a mountainous farm area in India. One of his intents was to explain why people adopt such a marriage system. Do all groups who practice polyandry do so for the same reasons? Can we find a universal explanation for this marriage pattern?

Westermarck (1894) suggested long ago that polyandry is a way of minimizing population growth to cope with scarce resources. Fraternal polyandry keeps brothers together and slows the growth of the family, since several brothers will produce only the number of children their one wife can bear. Tibet is a land of scarce resources and relatively little productive land. Goldstein agrees that fraternal polyandry minimizes the need to divide land and reduces the breakup of the family that is more likely to occur when each brother marries monogamously. It ensures the continuation of a single family as an economic unit.

Technically, any of the brothers in a polyandrous family in the groups studied by Goldstein could demand his share of family property and start his own, independent family. Certainly there were reasons why a younger brother might wish to do so. Within the polyandrous family, he was subordinate to his older brothers and experienced the brunt of intersibling tensions. As the younger husband, he had difficulty obtaining equal sexual access to his wife, particularly if the age difference between him and the eldest husband was great. Furthermore, a large age difference might also imply less compatibility between the younger brother and the wife. The youngest sibling, therefore, found himself in a psychologically undesirable and stressful situation. He was an economic hostage who was able to exercise little control over his situation.

In practice, however, younger sons rarely opted to go their own way. In spite of the psychological appeals such a choice might have had, the practical benefits of staying had still more appeal. First, the family itself opposed the desire to leave the polyandrous family as a form of economic disloyalty. After all, sharing a wife eliminated the cost of allocating family resources equally to each child. Furthermore, this type of marriage system had the advantage of producing only one set of heirs each generation. With the family land intact, all family members were able to experience a better quality of life and higher social status. Finally, those who did choose to leave the family unit to establish separate marriages lost membership in the corporate family and faced the costs of reestablishing themselves independently.

The personal costs of starting an independent family were perhaps the greatest deterrent to this choice. Until China took over Tibet in 1969, it was nearly impossible for younger brothers to leave the family corporation. Independent farming was not feasible due to the scarcity of good land. (Animal husbandry was equally unfeasible due to the high mortality rate of livestock.) Even if one did *not* want to marry polyandrously, few other good options existed. Polyandry was much more commonly a practice among the landowners than for the poor. Poorer families existed primarily through wage labor, crafts, or servitude, and a younger brother of a landowning family who chose to set up his own marriage and household was likely to become a member of this poorer social class.

Despite the potential drawbacks to polyandry, it does offer economic security, affluence, and social prestige. Families practicing polyandry do *not* do so merely to survive in the harsh Himalayan environment. Instead, the sharing of the estate and the establishment of a corporate identity allows them access to a "lifestyle of the rich and famous." Polyandry maximizes the families' potential to achieve affluence and desired material possessions. However, its benefits significantly decreased after China's takeover of Tibet. With the change in governments came an increase in trade with neighboring countries. Tibetans were then better able to earn a living away from the family land. New opportunities as traders allowed younger siblings to leave the restrictiveness of their stem family and to have a realistic chance of making it on their own. Consequently, a decrease in the polyandrous marriages and an increase in independent monogamous households occurred.

Goldstein compared the polyandry of Limi in Nepal to that of Pahari in India. Outwardly, polyandry in Pahari looks very much like polyandry in Tibet, and one finds the same diversity of marriages in both societies: monogamy, polygyny, and fraternal polyandry. However, the rate of fraternal polyandry occurrence was lower in Pahari, where group marriage was the most common family form. In Pahari prestige rose as the number of wives increased, so polygynous and polygynandrous families are desirable, since both kinds of marriage maximize the number of wives a man has. One barrier to increasing family size through marriage in Pahari was the requirement of paying a "brideprice" to the bride's family in compensation for its loss of her productive capacity. This contrasts with the practice in Tibet, where each new wife would bring a dowry into the marriage. Social status, esteem, and wealth result from the best of such polygynous marriages. Simple fraternal polyandry is resorted to by poorer families who can provide no more than one wife to be shared by brothers.

Among prosperous families in Pahari, it was the eldest brother who had the responsibility of finding wives for younger brothers. By combining polygyny and polyandry, he could obtain a second wife for himself and increase his own status while also providing a wife for his brothers. So polygyny combined with polyandry was increasingly practiced when favorable economic conditions prevailed. In contrast with Limi, where polyandry was practiced to amass wealth and prestige, Paharians practiced polyandry because second and subsequent males were too poor to pay a "brideprice" to obtain a wife.

Levine (1988) studied polyandry among the Nyinba, a group of ethnic Tibetans who live in the rugged Himalayan region of Northwestern Nepal. She points out that polyandry has profound effects on the social life and on domestic relations particularly. Westerners think of monogamy as the normal, even moral, form of marriage and portray men as naturally desiring multiple mates whom they wish to possess exclusively, so they have tended to see polyandry as an aberration that men would normally avoid. Those unfamiliar with polyandry might expect its domestic life to contrast with the male dominance that is common in polygynous marriages. But Levine noted that polyandry creates a family whose central core is a group of men, usually brothers, who emphasize their solidarity and control over society's economic life. Thus, polyandrous families are dominated by men, who are favored over women in "special systems of property inheritance and succession to positions of household authority" (p. 3). Another factor making polyandrous societies male-centered is that women leave home to live with their husbands on land that is inherited by sons.

The imbalance of men in the polyandrous family also has profound effects on gender roles, especially on the division of labor. In Nyinba "men specialize in subsistence activities, including long-distance trade, while their wives supervise agriculture in the village" (Levine, 1988, p. 3).

Since co-husbands are brothers, kinship reinforces their close emotional ties in Nyinba society. They see their economic interests as identical, and they define each other as equals who trust one another more than they can trust anyone else. Kinship determines one's status in the community at large and the kind of relationships one has with other members of the community. According to Levine, "Kinship proximity becomes important in securing the mutual commitments of co-husbands in polyandrous marriages it seems to be among the strongest motivations for cooperation in large Nyinba households" (p. 10).

Nyinba notions of kinship strongly emphasize the relationship between fathers and children. Each brother in the family thinks of himself as the "real" father of specific children. This provides the basis for organizing the community into larger groups of paternally related kin that emphasize social obligations that correspond with degrees of relatedness. Levine reports:

> For Nyinba, these notions about heredity and character also support practices of endogamy and a certain closure against the outside world.... It also supports a closed kinship calculus, which has no place for outsiders and reinforces a stance of ethnic separateness. Ethnic separateness, finally, justifies local and stratum endogamy and restrictions placed upon migration. (pp. 10-11)

The partitioning of kin against nonrelatives even operates within the community. For instance, the Nyinba distinguish between two social strata within their society: "the higher-ranked descendants of village founders, who are full citizens and landholders, and the lower-ranked descendants of their former slaves" (p. 11). Thus, Nyinba polyandry, like that of Tibet and India, implies the presence of important class distinctions. This point has been taken up by Schuler (1987). She has given the issue an important twist by examining an aspect of polyandry that has been long neglected by other researchers—the status of women in polyandrous societies.

Schuler studied polyandry in Chumik, a society in Tibet that is similar to those studied by Goldstein and Levine. Schuler asserts that an important element of polyandry is a large number of unmarried women: "In Chumik about 22% of women 35 years of age and above, and 28% of those age 45 and above have never been married" (p. 2). Although these figures correspond closely to rates of nonmarriage reported for other polyandrous societies, just what happens to these women has not been a topic of careful study. In fact, most studies of polyandry have been so caught up in discussing polyandry in terms of men, that the relevance of women's roles in explaining polyandry has been largely ignored.

A number of writers have noted that women in polyandrous Tibet appear to have an unusually high status compared with neighboring nonpolyandrous countries (Bell, 1928; Peissel, 1968). Unlike Islamic countries and India, polyandrous Tibetan men and women mix freely in public. There is no seclusion of women. Women seem to be vocal and influential. Thus, outsiders have assumed that their status was high. Indeed, the fact that they could have several husbands seemed to be evidence of their high status. Schuler claims that such a view incorrectly romanticizes the position of women in polyandrous Tibet. It ignores the implications that widespread nonmarriage has for the status of women in these societies.

In societies such as the Toda of southern India's Decan Plateau, female infanticide was a widespread way of eliminating the "surplus" of women that polyandry created (Rivers, 1906). In Tibet this was not the case. Instead, there were many adult unmarried women, whose economic roles were vital to their societies' adaptation to environments that demanded the labor of large numbers of agricultural workers.

According to Schuler, families in Chumik typically preferred a daughter as a first-born child, because a daughter can help her mother with work. Families prefer to keep daughters in the household as long as they can, because their daughters' labor is economically important. They adopt various strategies to keep their daughters unmarried so they can contribute work to the family. They may even demand that the in-laws allow a married daughter to return home to work during the day or for an extended period during each harvest season for several years after she marries. Chumikwa society frowns on remarriage after divorce or widowhood. Of course, polyandry itself makes it impossible for many women to marry.

Unmarried women engage in various income-producing trades, such as keeping a small inn, selling home-distilled liquor, or spinning and weaving textiles for income. Wealthy patron families often hire unmarried women for specific work. Seasonal agricultural labor is a scarce resource, and unmarried women are a labor pool for this work. According to Schuler, "Wage labor and labor exchange groups are comprised in large part of unmarried females" (p. 70). It is improper for unmarried women to refuse offers for temporary work by landowning families. Indeed, since they are generally poor, unmarried women can ill afford to refuse such work. Remaining single does offer women the opportunity for somewhat greater freedom than is enjoyed by married women. But the lot of unmarried women is a difficult one, and it is understandable that women do not generally choose that state.

Since a family's land is inherited by its sons but worked by women, daughters who do not marry become part of the lower social class of landless workers, a class Chumikwans generally describe as descendants of earlier slaves. The harsh life of unmarried women helps to maintain the more comfortable lifestyle and higher social standing of landowning men and their wives. Unmarried women pass on their low social position to any children they may have, since their children are defined as illegitimate. So the lower class labor pool perpetuates itself, largely through the downward social movement of a large percentage of women each generation and through the addition of any children they may bear.

■ References

Bell, C. (1928). *The people of Tibet*. Oxford: Clarendon Press.

Levine, N. E. (1988). *The dynamics of polyandry: Kinship, domesticity, and population on the Tibetan border*. Chicago: University of Chicago Press.

Levine, N. E., & Sangree, W. H. (1980). Conclusion: Asian and African systems of polyandry. *Journal of Comparative Family Studies, 11*, 385-410.

Goldstein, M.C. (1979). Pahari and Tibetan polyandry revisited. *Ethnology, 17*, 325-337.

Peissel, M. (1968). *Mustang: A lost Tibetan kingdom.* London: Collins and Harvill.

Rivers, W. H. R. (1906). *The Todas.* New York: Macmillan.

Schuler, S. R. (1987). *The other side of polyandry: Property, stratification, and nonmarriage in the Nepal Himalayas.* Boulder, CO: Westview Press.

Westermarck, E. R. (1894). *The history of human marriage* (3 vols.). New York: Macmillan. (Original work published 1891)

■ Discussion Questions

1.   What social pressures do Tibetan individuals face in their culture regarding who, when, and where to marry?

2.   There appears to be a definite pecking order in a polyandrous marriage based on age. From this report or other studies of sibling birth order, what can you conclude about the position of the youngest brother in such marriages?

3.   What contrasts between Pahari and Tibet make the role of polyandry different for these two places?

■ For Further Exploration

1.   American culture prefers monogamous marriages that form their own independent households, often in places distant from the parents of either spouse. Discuss how this might be a social adaptation to our industrialized technology. Explain how an employment system in which we do not inherit our occupations and means of livelihood from our parents could encourage this marriage preference. Can you also relate the low esteem in which the American elderly are held to these economic facts and to our marriage and household residence patterns?

■ For Additional Reading

Levine, N. E. (1988). *The dynamics of polyandry: Kinship, domesticity, and population on the Tibetan border.* Chicago: University of Chicago Press. An examination of cultural and social factors in polyandry among the Nyinba of Northwestern Nepal.

Schuler, S. R. (1987). *The other side of polyandry: Property, stratification, and nonmarriage in the Nepal Himalayas.* Boulder, CO: Westview Press. An analysis of polyandrous marriage and the economic role of unmarried women in Chumik, Tibet.

The Berdache: Gender-Mixing Among Northern Native Americans

■ Stimulus Questions

Under what circumstances would a person be expected to assume the dress and/or social functions of the opposite sex? How might such a switch in gender roles be related to a person's sexual activity?

AMONG many Northern American groups, *berdaches* represented a gender intermediate between male and female (Callender & Kochems, 1983; Jacobs, 1968). A berdache is a person who adopts the dress or occupation or behavior (or any combination thereof) of members of the opposite sex, thereby acquiring a distinct gender status. The berdache gender was most common among Native Americans living in the western region of the United States and Canada. It was usually assumed by males—as many as 113 different tribes recognized the berdache gender for males—but female berdaches were reported in at least 30 tribes. Early accounts of berdaches go back to the sixteenth century, and they still exist today, although rather covertly, since Western attitudes have discouraged the practice of berdache roles.

Male berdaches usually dressed as women and female berdaches as men in most tribes, but there was variation. For instance, the Pima forbade cross-dressing, but expected the berdache to imitate the speech, behavior, and postures of the opposite sex. Among the Navajo, the berdache would dress as a man to do work usually done by men (for example, warfare or silver working) and as a woman to do the work that women normally did (for example, carrying firewood or textile working). Some societies, such as the Paiute, Wintu, and Shoshoni, allowed individuals to choose whether they dressed as male or female.

The berdache did not typically adopt all the roles of the opposite sex. Instead, he or she combined certain roles assigned to both genders and thereby achieved a distinctive gender status. The culture of each society in which the berdache was found defined exactly which of the traditional roles of each gender were to be adopted by the berdache. So there was much variation in how a berdache was expected to act in different North American groups (Davis & Whitten, 1987, p. 84). For some, the cross-dressing was complete, for others, only partial or nonexistent. In some tribes, the berdache was expected to behave heterosexually, in others, bisexually, homosexually, or asexually. Probably the most consistent expectation was that the berdache would frequently participate in economic activities that were normally performed by members of the opposite sex.

In most Native American societies that had them, the berdaches played an important part in the religious life. Often, they were religious healers who cared for the sick. Among the Teton and the Tewa, berdaches named children at christening ceremonies. California berdaches were responsible for burial and mourning rituals. Among Plains tribes, it was commonly believed that a berdache could give supernatural support to a raid by accompanying the warriors. The religious element of the berdache status was also expressed in the idea shared by many tribes that a person might be called to berdache status through a vision. The creation stories of the Southwestern Native Americans portrayed the first humans as berdaches.

Information about berdache sexual behavior is limited, partly due to the sensitivity of the topic, but also because it is difficult to describe the customs of a society that recognizes three or even four genders in the language of a society that has terms for only two. For instance, most accounts of Plains Indian berdache sexual activity say that berdaches married homosexually. However, berdaches were typically not permitted to enter relationships with one another. So berdache sexual customs in that society involved sexual relations between persons of the same biological but different societally defined gender. On the other hand, Navajo and Shoshoni berdaches usually married someone of the opposite biological gender, although they might have sexual relations with both men and women outside marriage. Tewa Pueblo berdaches were expected to be bisexual, but again did not have relationships with other berdaches. And Zuni Pueblo berdaches were expected to be asexual, since they were thought to embody both masculine and feminine elements in one person and to have no need for a mate to complete themselves. Ingalik berdaches were also consistently described as asexual.

Although accounts vary greatly from tribe to tribe, sexual relationships between berdaches and others ranged from casual, promiscuous encounters to stable marriages. The Santee and Teton Dakota allowed promiscuity but did not support long-term sexual relationships or marriage. Among the Crow, female berdaches often married women, but few male berdaches chose to marry. A male Hidatsa berdache could marry and adopt children by whom he would be called "mother," and female berdache "husbands" of some tribes would sometimes hire non-berdache males to impregnate their wives.

The institution of the berdache is easily misunderstood by people brought up in Western cultures in which the berdache did not exist. Early accounts often refered to berdaches as "hermaphrodites," a notion that is clearly incorrect, since there were far too many berdaches in societies where they were recognized to be accounted for by such a rare biological phenomenon. Similarly, sexual orientation fails to account for the berdache. The sexual behavior of berdaches was not consistent from tribe to tribe, and was too diverse throughout North America to be a defining element of the berdache status itself. In some groups, parents selected a child to become a berdache while it was still an infant. Informed studies also indicate that even in those societies in which adolescents adopted berdache roles, homosexual behavior seems to have been secondary to the gender change rather than a cause of it.

Some early theorists suggested that the male berdache status was simply an avenue for less aggressive young men who were not inclined to the role of warrior. Yet many non-warlike tribes, such as those of the Great Basin, recognized the berdache status, and many warlike groups did not. Additionally, some warlike tribes accepted berdaches as persons of high social rank, while belittling non-berdache men who were thought to fear warfare. When U.S. soldiers attempted to enter the village of Zuni in 1892 to arrest one of the Zuni war chiefs, it was a male berdache, described as the "tallest and strongest" of the tribe who took the lead in resisting the soldiers (Roscoe, 1991, pp. 104-110). None of this suggests that male berdaches typically entered their status to avoid the rigors of the male role. In fact, berdaches accompanied warriors to battle for various functions. Cheyenne berdaches treated the wounded, had custody of scalps, and organized the dance that followed a raid. The Teton Dakota consulted their berdaches for success in battle. The success of a war party was sometimes attributed to the inclusion of a berdache.

One theory of how people became berdaches emphasizes the economic roles that such a role made available. The berdache was particularly common in societies where men and women provided different, but equally important, incomes to their families. For instance, among the Plains Indians, women tended the gardens that provided the staple foods of corn, beans, and squash, while men hunted game animals, such as the bison that provided not only meat, but hides, sinews, and bones that were used for making important tools. A family that lacked a child of either sex might raise a son or daughter as a berdache who could provide the economic benefits they would otherwise have had to forego. Children's interest in and aptitude for the work of the opposite sex might lead them into the life of a berdache. Male berdaches were exceptionally skilled in women's work including cooking, housework, crafts, and plant gathering. Likewise, female berdaches showed a propensity for hunting and military exploits. Because of the economic benefits that the berdache provided, the status was a respected one. For instance, the Navajo, among whom the berdache could produce the income of both a man and a woman, regarded a family with a berdache as particularly fortunate, one that would be assured of wealth.

After adulthood the economic benefits of the berdache persisted. Households based on a marriage between a man and a male berdache or between a woman and a female berdache were generally very well-to-do. For example, among the various Plains tribes the highest-status men were warriors who were successful enough in the work of men that they could provide for several wives, berdache men usually married into such an existing heterosexual marriage, forming a higher status polygamous family and an economically more flexible household at the same time. Through a second marriage to a male berdache, a young, aspiring warrior could rise socially more quickly than would have been possible otherwise. A berdache wife who could cooperate with her husband in men's work or with her co-wife in women's work was very valuable.

U.S. culture has no formally recognized and accepted equivalent of the berdache. Traditional American concepts of gender reflect only the biological distinction between male and female. Cultural beliefs about the dominant and aggressive nature of males and the submissive, nurturing qualities of females have been supported by the legal acceptance of only heterosexual relationships. So behaviors and lifestyles that do not fit readily into this dichotomy have been stigmatized, especially those that have challenged the dominant role of men over women. Nevertheless, in recent times, as the economic lives of American men and women have become more similar, Americans have at least informally developed some acceptance of berdache-like alternatives. For instance, the recent concept of androgynous persons as those who have more fully developed both the "masculine" and "feminine" sides of themselves clearly parallels the concept of the berdache. The modern Western concept of "sexual orientation" also expresses an awareness that relationships are not simply an expression of a single inborn norm. So perhaps the Native American concept of three or more genders is less alien to U.S. culture today than it was a generation ago.

■ References

Callender. C., & Kochems, L. M. (1983). The North American berdache. *Current Anthropology*, *24*, 443-470.

Davis, D. L., & Whitten, R. G. (1987). The cross-cultural study of human sexuality. *Annual Review of Anthropology, 1987*. Annual Reviews.

Jacobs, S. (1968). Berdache: A brief review of the literature. *Colorado Anthropologist*, *1*, 25-40.

Roscoe, W. (1991). *The Zuni man-woman*. Albuquerque, NM: University of New Mexico Press.

■ Discussion Questions

1.   What misconceptions exist regarding the origin of the berdache?

2.   How did the berdache differ from American bisexuality or homosexuality?

3.   If gays and lesbians were granted the right to formalize their relationships as legal marriages, would homosexual marriages then be best understood as a variety of the berdache? Why or why not?

4.   Discuss sexual behaviors and/or orientations that in our culture are largely acceptable or unacceptable. What determines whether society is willing to tolerate them?

■ For Further Exploration

1.   What issues does the institution of the berdache raise for the definition of homosexuality and bisexuality in American culture? Would being homosexual, lesbian, bisexual, or heterosexual be better understood as matters of biological gender, psychology, or both?

■ For Additional Reading

Blackwood, E. (1986). *The many faces of homosexuality: Anthropological approaches to homosexual behavior.* New York: Harrington Park Press. This exceptional collection of articles includes several on berdache-like statuses in a variety of societies throughout the world.

Nanda, S. (1990). *Neither man nor woman: The Hijras of India.* Belmont, CA: Wadsworth. An engrossing account of a berdache-like religious group in contemporary India.

Cross-Cultural Differences in Sexual Jealousy

■ Stimulus Questions

Are there cultures in which people do not experience jealousy, or do people get jealous in every society? Would flirting with someone cause jealousy in Russia or Yugoslavia just as it might in the United States?

ACCORDING to Ford and Beach (1951, pp. 115-116), only 53% of societies studied by anthropologists have rules that forbid extramarital sex by both husbands and wives. Anthropologists noted long ago that there are a number of societies that permit or even encourage sexual relationships that Americans would probably respond to with jealousy. For instance, according to Rivers (1906), the Toda of the southern Decan Plateau of India considered it inappropriate for a man to refuse a wife's request to have an affair with another man. He was expected to show no jealousy over such a relationship. Do such examples mean that jealousy is not experienced in all societies or that people can overcome it readily if they are socialized appropriately? Perhaps not.

Reiss (1986, pp. 45-80) has asserted that all human societies are aware of sexual jealousy in marriage and have cultural rules for handling it. Hupka (1981) made a cross-cultural study of jealousy in 92 societies and found that the more important marriage was thought to be, the more jealousy people showed. In Reiss's view, jealousy exists in all societies, but people express it more readily in some societies than in others. The effect of expressed jealousy is to define the boundaries of the group within which sexual relationships are permissible. So when marriage is very important for people's survival and well-being as adults, their culture will encourage the expression of jealousy. According to Reiss, the expression of jealousy by men and women is also influenced by their relative amount of social power: Women are less likely to express jealousy in societies in which they have little social power in comparison with men. In the world's more egalitarian societies, women have greater social power and more readily express their jealousy.

Cultures seem to differ not only in how much jealousy people show and in who is likely to show it, but also in which behaviors seem to trigger it. In many cultures marriages and sexual relationships are strictly regulated by concepts of kinship that are not relevant to relationships in the United States. For instance, many societies, such as the ancient Hebrews, required a man to marry his deceased brother's widow, a custom called the *levirate*. In some of these societies where the levirate was practiced, an affair between a man's wife and his younger brother during his lifetime was not considered to be grounds for jealousy. However, the opposite circumstance, an affair between a man and his younger brother's wife was grounds for jealousy.

Among the Nayar of India, a husband and wife did not always share a common residence, and the husband would visit his wife at her residence. She would conceive most of her children by various men with whom she had short-term relationships. This was no basis for jealousy by the primary husband, who had no say in her choice of other sexual partners. He might, however, express jealousy if his wife displayed a lack of interest in him—either sexually or nonsexually—in their personal relationship.

Probably the most common triggers of jealousy are sexual behaviors, but the specific type of behavior that elicits sexual jealousy varies from culture to culture. You and I have an idea of how we might react or feel seeing our partner and a third person kissing, hugging, or dancing together. If sexual jealousy, or some degree of jealousy, is our response, would people elsewhere in the world respond similarly? Might a behavior, such as flirting, have a similar meaning and elicit similar feelings regardless of culture? It also seems reasonable that a behavior that is legitimate and not threatening in one culture would not be viewed so favorably in another. The context in which a behavior takes place and the meanings assigned to that behavior affect the interpretation given to it, which then becomes the trigger for an emotional response.

Buunk and Hupka (1987) examined behaviors eliciting sexual jealousy in seven different industrialized nations: Hungary, Ireland, Mexico, the Netherlands, the Soviet Union, the United States, and Yugoslavia. The researchers asked over 2,000 students with a mean age of 20 or 21 years, to rate a series of questions regarding behaviors such as "When my lover dances with someone else I feel very uneasy," or "It does not bother me when I see my lover flirting with someone else." Students indicated their level of agreement or disagreement on a 7-point Likert-type scale. Mean scores were then calculated for each behavior to indicate whether that particular behavior actually did elicit jealousy. Comparisons were made across countries to see how universal or culture-specific such phenomena were.

Men and women differed only in their reactions to their partners' kissing and sexual fantasies. In all nations, women reported a greater degree of jealousy than men about kissing. On the other hand, men in all countries were more negative about their partners expressing sexual fantasies about someone outside their relationship. Men and women indicated similar levels of jealousy regarding flirting by their partner. Both sexes gave neutral responses for dancing and hugging in all the societies studied. Both men and women in all cultures responded negatively to sexual relationships between a partner with another person.

There were significant national differences for all the different jealousy factors. No one country was always more positive or more negative than the others. The Yugoslavians reacted with the most jealousy to flirting. Of all the nations, however, they showed the lowest level of jealousy toward kissing. Students from Hungary reacted in the opposite way. They expressed very little jealousy about flirting but quite a lot about kissing. Dancing and hugging were not viewed as personal threats in any country.

Regarding sexual relationships, the Soviets expressed the most jealousy of all the countries. Mexicans were less jealous than people of other nationalities except in regard to sexual relationships. The most jealous responses to sexual fantasies came from the Netherlands, but even there the typical reaction was fairly mild although, as mentioned, men were more bothered by their partners' fantasies than were women.

In this research on sexual jealousy, the researcher found more similarities than differences among these industrialized nations. Cross-culturally, flirting and sexual relationships were the consistent causes of jealousy. However, there were some cultural differences in which acts caused the most jealousy. In non-Western cultures, the exact behaviors that caused sexual jealousy varied more markedly, but it seems there are actions in any society that evoke jealousy even if it is not considered appropriate to express that jealousy.

■ References

Buunk, B., & Hupka, R. B. (1987). Cross-cultural differences in the elici-
    tation of sexual jealousy. *Journal of Sex Research*, *23*, 12-22.

Ford, C. S., & Beach, F. A. (1951). *Patterns of sexual behavior*. New
    York: Harper & Row.

Hupka, R. B. (1981). Cultural determinants of jealousy. *Alternative Life-
    styles*, *4*, 310-356.

Reiss, I. R. (1986). *Journey into sexuality: An exploratory voyage.*
    Englewood Cliffs, NJ: Prentice-Hall.

Rivers, W. H. R. (1906). *The Todas*. New York: Macmillan.

■ Discussion Questions

1.   How do differences in our expression of jealousy in casual dating,
     steady dating, engagements, and marriages support Reiss's idea
     that the role of jealousy is to define the boundaries of the group
     within which sexuality is permissible?

2.   What general conclusions can you draw about behaviors that elicit
     sexual jealousy from Buunk and Hupka's study of seven countries?

■ For Further Exploration

1.   Take the sexual jealousy questions used by Buunk and Hupka and
     conduct a small survey of students at your school. (The original
     article is available through most university libraries.) Does the data
     from your sample correspond with that reported by the authors for
     American students?

■ For Additional Reading

Frayser, S. G. (1985). *Varieties of sexual experience: An anthropoogical
    perspective on human sexuality*. New Haven, CT: Human Resource
    Area Files Press. A cross-cultural examination of human sexuality.